MAYDAY!

MAYDAY!

MAYDAY!

Charles Coleman

Copyright © 1995   Word Professionals Publishing
Honolulu, Hawaii 96820-0893
United States of America

This book is sold *as is*, without any kind of either expressed or implied warranty respecting the contents of this book, including but not limited to implied warranties for the book's quality, performance, or fitness for any particular purpose. Neither the author nor the publisher shall be liable to any person or entity with respect to any loss, or damage caused or alleged to be caused directly or indirectly by this book.

Library of Congress Cataloging-in Publication Data

Coleman, Charles.
  MAYDAY! MAYDAY! MAYDAY! / Charles Coleman.
     p. cm.
  ISBN 0-9634022-1-8
     1. *Haleakala* (Catamaran) 2. Coleman, Charles--Journeys. 3. Survival after airplane accidents, shipwrecks, etc. 4. Search and rescue operations. I. Title.
G530.H18C65 1995
910.4'5--dc20   92-27856
                                                                                      CIP

Printed in the United States of America

10 9 8 7 6 5 4 3 2 1

Word Professionals Publishing
P. O. Box 30893
Honolulu, Hawaii 96820-0893

ii

This book is dedicated to Sadie.

Contents

Acknowledgements

I quite literally owe my life to the people of the maritime search and rescue system.

This book is intended to be an expression of support for the United States Coast Guard, the United States Air Force, and the National Oceanic and Atmospheric Administration Search and Rescue forces, both dedicated and voluntary. My special gratitude goes to the particular individuals of these organizations who helped rescue me, and the ham operators of the amateur radio service who helped me communicate my distress.

A great deal of information and insight is a key part of the tremendous adventure of survival on the high seas. I have learned much from the people who were involved and from others who have offered sailing and survival advice, especially after they heard this story. Even without being able to cite the specific individual sources, I hope to pass on much of what I have learned to be valuable for survival at sea.

This book details my own experience and my analysis of the rescue mission based on U.S. government publications and public records. I have reproduced greatly reduced and edited copies of the Defense Mapping Agency Chart 541 and information extracted from the National Search and Rescue Manual and the SAR Case File for *Haleakala* including various non-classified wires recorded in the case file. I have freely edited and re-expressed the information, primarily expanding and replacing abbreviations and acronyms to make the meaning more intelligible to a wider audience.

My deepest appreciation and love go to my wife who suffered through this terrible ordeal and whose participation was a key element in the rescue effort. Later she helped make this book a reality through encouragement, prodding, goading, and finally through preparation and editing of the manuscript.

Preface

It took some time after being rescued before I could face writing about my survival. I suppose it was the pain of reliving the events while writing about them. Then, as the work progressed and the chapters were filled in, what had at first been painful became a catharsis. Now when I am first introduced to someone or a stranger approaches me, I'm often asked the same set of questions. I'll use this opportunity to answer in print.

Is it a true story?

The story that you are about to read is absolutely true in all facts and details as well as I can remember and could determine from the records of the events.

Were you afraid of sharks?

Yes, I was afraid of sharks and the question of shark attack is addressed in the book.

What happened to Sadie?

Please read the book to find out what happened to Sadie. To try to explain in a few words would do injustice.

Do you still sail?

Yes, I still get great pleasure from sailing.

Would you build another boat?

I probably would build another boat, but not by doing all of the work myself (and Elli might voice strong objections).

Many have asked to read the manuscript before publication and two more questions often arise from initially flipping through the pages.

Why so many footnotes?

The large number of footnotes is unusual, particularly in a non-technical book. They are used to include much detail, both fact and opinion, which is important to the situation but not necessarily to the story. Set off as footnotes you have the option to include or ignore this additional information.

Why have you included documents in a story of survival?

Originally I assumed that the more technically minded readers, and particularly those new to sailing, would enjoy the official documentation while others would skip both the footnotes and documents to follow the narrative. Sailors, even very experienced blue-water sailors, have confirmed that they learned much and greatly appreciated the detail. Surprisingly, comments from a number of non-technical non-sailors suggest that these documents can make fascinating reading because they show behind-the-scenes of a rescue mission.

MAYDAY!

MAYDAY!

MAYDAY!

To Venture Forth

In the quiet darkness of the wee hours before dawn, I was busy preparing for an overnight single-handed sail between two of the American Samoan islands. It was autumn in the Southern Hemisphere, the end of the cyclone season and the time for cruising sailors to venture forth from safe harbor. Still early April, it was also the time for voyages northward because the Northern Hemisphere hurricane season would not return again for several more months.

Haleakala was anchored in Pago Pago harbor, the great "hurricane hole" of the South Pacific. My destination was the small boat harbor on Ofu in the Manu'a Island Group. This overnight trip was to be a shakedown cruise in preparation for a month-long single-handed sail to Honolulu. Should all systems perform as well as anticipated, I intended to bypass Manu'a and continue on to Hawaii.

The 56-foot sailing catamaran *Haleakala* had been my home for several years and now was fully provisioned, with stores more than sufficient for at least twice the time that the trip to Honolulu should take.

The designs of most vessels, including *Haleakala*, give the feeling of sacrificing comfort space for seaworthiness. Even at that, *Haleakala* had enough room to be justly compared to a

Figure 1 **Charley and Elli aboard *Haleakala* in Pago Pago Harbor.**

compact house. The original design[1] provided for six bedrooms (staterooms) and four were outfitted with queen sized beds while the remaining two currently were being used for storage. The two bathrooms (heads), were each located centrally between a pair of staterooms in either hull. Also more typical of a small house than a large boat, many appliances were installed aboard, including a microwave/browner oven, refrigerator/freezer, dishwasher, clothes washer, etc..[2]

---

[1]See the construction drawing reproduced as Figure 8, on page 40.

[2]The size of the vessel can be approximated by noting that the crown of the cabin top is at shoulder height in Figure 1. The large size of the vessel is then more apparent in the view taken from the shore in Tonga and shown as Figure 2.

Figure 2 *Haleakala* at anchor in Tonga.

A number of changes had been made to the vessel with an eye to increasing safety while making a long, single-handed voyage easier. The total amount of Diesel oil had been more than doubled to extend the range under power. Temporary fuel tanks, made from two 55-gallon drums and mounted near the steering pedestal, augmented the 80 gallon built-in capacity to 190 gallons, plus 60 gallons in emergency cans (approximately a 2000 mile range without the emergency supply). A new Satellite Navigation (SATNAV) system had been installed. The rigging had been thoroughly checked and tuned. The dinghy was in place on its new mount on the aft deck where it could be more quickly and easily launched than from its previous position lashed to the forward net. All gear was stowed, and I was prepared to depart.

Proper charts are an essential part of safe sailing, and with nearly 250 charts aboard, the vessel could have sailed to almost any part of the world. However, I also knew from prior passages that even the latest charts are not necessarily complete and accurate, and some of the most recently published charts of Pacific islands were often considerably out of date. For instance, the latest chart of Christmas Island, which was well placed on the planned course to consider for a stopover, still showed lighted buoys on the approach to the inner lagoon. Yet on the first stop there by *Haleakala*, years ago, no one we talked to on the island could remember there ever having been such navigation lights or buoys marking the entrance channel.

All the proper charts covering the voyage to Hawaii were assembled and were checked for dates and coverage. On top of the stack was Chart 541 of the Defense Mapping Agency covering the entire area between Samoa and Hawaii. Rhumb lines were plotted from Pago Pago to Honolulu and from Pago Pago to Ofu to Christmas Island to Honolulu as shown in Figure 3. The rhumb lines thus form a triangle with Pago Pago, Christmas Island and Hawaii at the vertices.[3] Underneath 541 were all of the individual larger-scale charts of the areas on the sail plan, and they appeared to be in order, with the exception of the chart for my initial destination, the small harbor on Ofu.

---

[3]The chart, itself, is much larger than the reproduced image in the figure. The original is almost four and a half feet tall. Although the details of the chart are illegible, the Hawaiian Island Group is easily identified in the upper right corner and the Samoan Group appears in the lower left corner. The Equator is approximately half way down the chart and although unmarked, lies just below Christmas Island which is marked by the mid-right vertex of the plotted triangle.

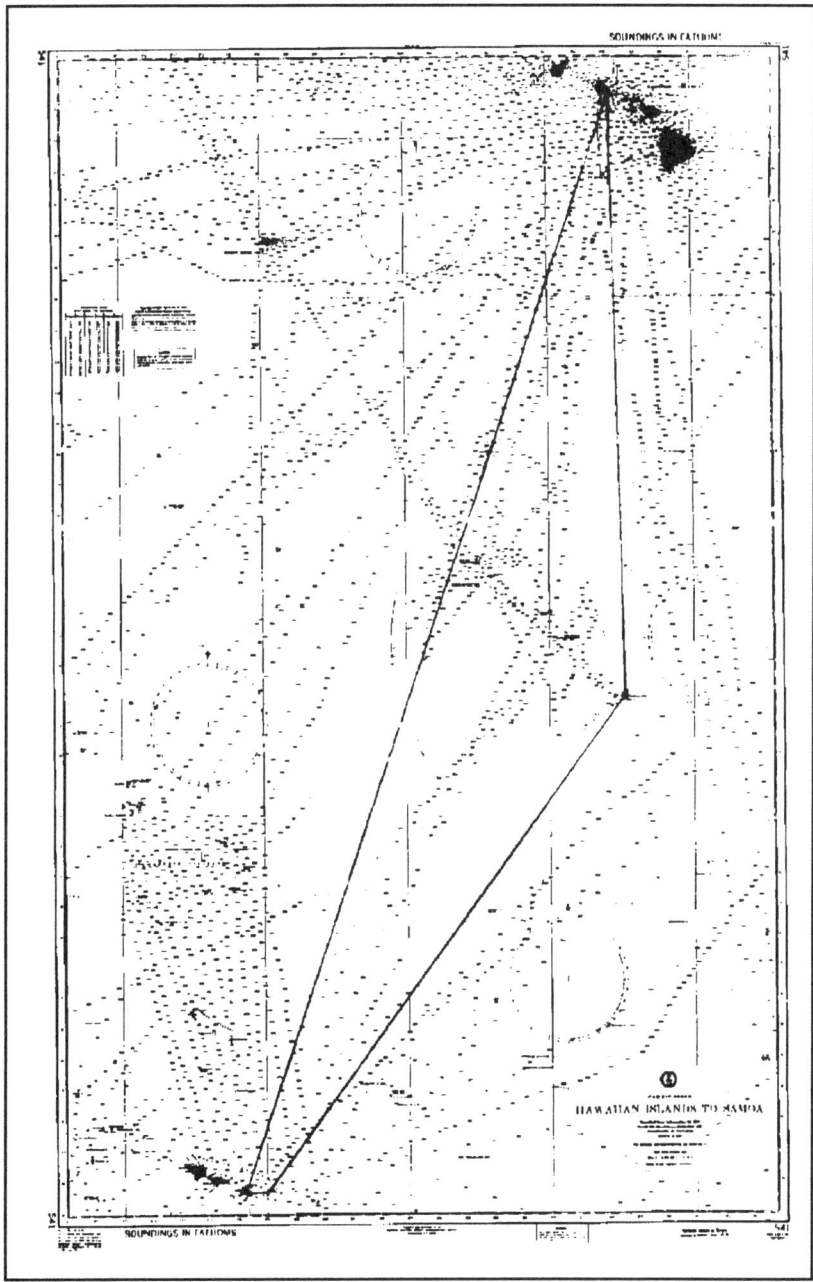

Figure 3   **The geographic limits for the planned voyage.**

Maneuvering in such a tight space could be difficult for a vessel of the size of *Haleakala*. I therefore discussed my sail plan with Herb Hoover, Chief of Ports Engineering for the Government of American Samoa. We updated a copy of the Manu'a islands chart with new details and cautions so I could enter and depart the harbor safely.

As was my custom prior to getting underway, I went over each point on my Sailing Checklist,[4] a one-page list of all the items I thought important to verify before getting underway.

I found this checklist invaluable, particularly when there were people aboard who were unfamiliar with *Haleakala*. It also served as a reminder of things that might easily be overlooked even with crew that had sailed with me before and who were familiar with the boat. For example, the majority of the safety check items addressed equipment important to new people aboard, like reviewing the location and use of the anchors, how to operate the radios to get help in an emergency, etc.. The one item I considered most important on the safety equipment list was the verification that everyone aboard, including myself, carried at least the minimum essential personal safety equipment—a knife, a whistle, and a small strobe or flashlight.[5]

---

[4]The list was divided into three sections and placed inside a plastic sheet protector so a grease pencil could be used to check off each item before each sail. The check list covered: 1) sail and engine checks, 2) safety equipment checks, and 3) "getting underway" items, such as checking freshwater tank levels and disconnecting shore power.

[5]In addition, because of the difficulty of using a strobe for anything other than attracting attention, both a small strobe <u>and</u> a flashlight are minimal items of personal safety equipment I now carry and recommend.

When I reached that item on the list, I put my knife and whistle around my neck on a lanyard and slipped a waterproof flashlight in my pocket, clipping its lanyard to my belt. Even when single-handing, the checklist was an important reminder for me.

The checklist also covered my own safety regulations known to past crews as "Charley's Rules." One of Charley's Rules required shoes be worn at all times, except when bathing or sleeping, and thongs were recommended when bathing. This rule was made as a precaution to prevent dislocated or broken toes, a painful and common occurrence aboard small vessels at sea. I still consider shoes a part of safety gear.

The checklist was completed just after dawn and the engine was started. At the sound of the engine, Sadie, who had been following me around as I checked the things on the list, immediately disappeared below. She hated the engine noise and knew we were about to get underway.

Sadie Thompson, a beautiful calico cat, was born under the house of a doctor in Pago Pago, and named after the famous woman of ill repute in *Rain* by W. Somerset Maugham. Sadie had become a very sure-footed boat cat after having fallen into the water several times as a kitten. She definitely had a mind of her own and knew how to get around any rules that were established. For instance, one of the rules forbade cats on tables or galley counters, but Sadie found a way to skirt the rules. She begged and begged to be allowed to sit on the gently vibrating washing machine which was built into the end of the counter in the main salon. Once having established her right to be there, she then continually tried to extend her territory to cover the

Figure 4 **Young Sadie Thompson explores a pandanus leaf basket.**

whole counter space. If she was caught by surprise somewhere else on top of the counter, she'd dash across to the washer and "tag-up" like a baseball player. Sometimes she'd even keep one back paw safely on the washer "base" while stretching as far as she could to explore interesting items on the counter.

Sadie was definitely Elli's cat when we were anchored. Had my wife, Elli, not flown on ahead to Honolulu, Sadie would have sought her out aboard ship when the engine started. As a kitten her favorite place to sleep had been curled around Elli's neck, an uncomfortable arrangement in the tropics, and Elli would wake up and complain: "Who needs a fur collar in Pago Pago?" Although Sadie did not make a fur collar for me while at sea, she did become my shipboard shadow.

14

Haleakala

Haleakala set sail from Pago Pago in excellent weather with the long-range forecast for continuing good weather. While prepared to sail through severe weather, as all ocean sailors must be, I still made it a rule never to leave port in heavy weather or with heavy weather predicted. I was prepared for storms, and I had braved storms at sea, but I did not seek them out.

As we[6] motored down the channel of Pago Pago Harbor, I put on my safety harness with its two safety lines. From this point on I would have the harness on and clipped to a stationary object on the vessel all of the time on deck until we were finally safely anchored at our destination.[7]

---

[6]When I speak of "we" on this trip, I refer to myself and Sadie. Although, it's true I did not insist she wear whistle, knife, light, and shoes as I usually required of everyone else aboard, her companionship deserved at least passenger status if not even crew member status aboard *Haleakala*.

[7]The safety harness is the standard gear worn by sailors in blue water. For some it may be the only item worn while deep at sea. It is made of very strong nylon webbing with a closing strap which usually fastens with a double D-ring buckle. A third larger D-ring is securely attached to the front of the harness to serve as the anchor for two independent safety lines which, in turn, are securely spliced in place. Lastly, a snap shackle is securely spliced into the far end of each safety line.

The two safety lines permit safe free movement on deck by alternately unfastening one safety line and then refastening it to a strong point in a new location along the direction one wants to proceed before repeating the process with the other safety line. By always keeping at least one of the two lines

(continued...)

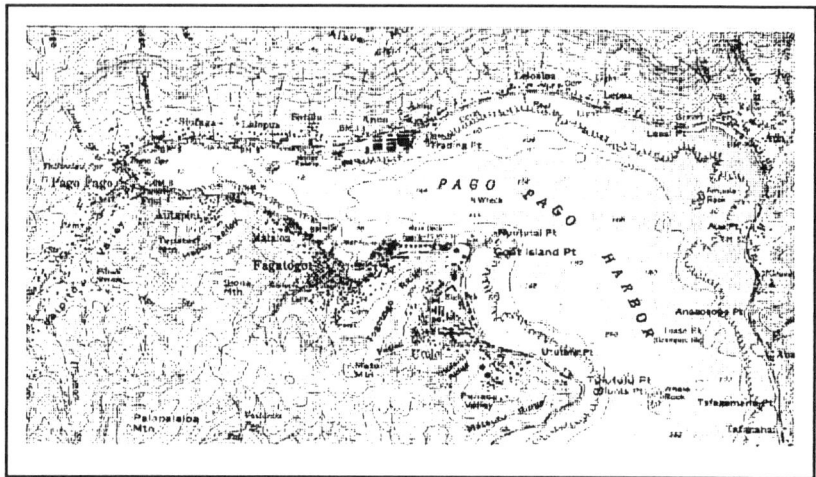

Figure 5   **Chart Detail of Pago Pago Harbor Showing Fagatoga.**

Pago Pago harbor is known as a deep water "hurricane hole" because of the great protection it provides in cyclone season. The basin is part of a volcanic caldera whose dog-leg shape and steep surrounding walls protect the harbor. The high mountains also create a local weather pattern. Innumerable small squalls sweep almost constantly through the harbor spawned by Mount Pioa, "Rainmaker mountain," which stands majestically to the east of the harbor entrance. This morning Rainmaker was again active, making rain from the moist South Pacific trade winds blowing from the east southeast, a little further to the east than the typical southeast Trade Winds. The small showers washed over the tuna canneries on the north shore of the harbor.

As we passed the canneries and headed south out of the harbor, I readied and set the mainsail and jib. Although these

_____

[7](...continued)
fastened to the vessel, the chances of being accidently lost overboard were essentially eliminated.

16

sails partially filled, I kept the engine running to compensate for the capricious winds that usually blow from different directions around the high cliffs surrounding the entrance.

Clearing the harbor mouth, we swung around due east to pass between the island of Tutuila and its tiny offshore companion, Aunu'u Island. We were so close hauled that the sails were used mostly to steady the boat while the engine provided the forward propulsion.

As we cleared Aunu'u and Tutuila, I hoisted the mizzen and changed course to the northeast allowing the sails to catch more wind and accelerate the boat although still close hauled. I stopped the engine, checked the set and adjusted the trim of the sails, and then went below to make breakfast. While Sadie and I sat down to our first meal underway, I entered our departure in the Captain's Log and plotted our course.

The wind was almost due east, which meant our present course passed well to the north of our destination. Under these conditions the plan was to sail until the island of Ofu was dead abeam, and then tack back about 100 to 110 degrees, leaving one final tack on the approach to the harbor.

It was smooth sailing as the hours wore on. Understandably, I was all keyed up at the beginning of a single-handed voyage, but I took extra care not to let my natural excitement cause me to overlook anything that needed attention. The rigging was a good place to start. I concentrated on the running rigging and found some fittings that needed to be replaced.

Solo sailing allows one to be much more in touch with the boat than when sailing with a large crew. Alone it is easier to notice things that had been fixed, or in some cases not fixed, by crew without my knowledge. I was not surprised to find that there were additional repairs to be checked out. Most of these small repairs were made the way I would have made them, and there had been no reason for crew to inform me of them.

I noticed the swivel shackle fiddle block[8] on the main sheet had been attached to the cabin top bail with a chain made of three shackles of assorted sizes. I assumed the original shackle holding it had been twisted or otherwise damaged and was replaced with shackles from the "helm supply,"[9] which I always kept handy on a deep shelf just inside the cabin door. Apparently three shackles had been used because no single one of the helm supply was the right size to be used alone. I went below, got out the box of assorted running rigging fittings, and selected a shackle of the correct size and shape. Then, by rigging a vang to parallel the main sheet, it was possible without dropping the main, to replace the three shackles with the single one of the proper size.

---

[8]Regardless of the native language spoken, sailor's also have a "seaman's language" that is largely composed of the words for the parts of a boat and the equipment aboard. This language allows rapid, unambiguous orders to be given but only if the listener understands the language. Therefore the seaman's terminology which follows will be readily understood by sailors although it may seem unintelligible to others. The applicable terms are used with apologies and footnotes for non-sailors.

[9]Over a period of time, small items that were found to be particularly handy, were collected on the helm supply shelf. It included such items as extra flashlights, rigging tape (to guard against chaffing), surveyor's marking tape (for wind direction tell-tales), snatch blocks, etc..

By early the next morning Manu'a Island was abeam. The prominent island of Ta'u was clearly visible, with Ofu and Olosega lying just to the west.

The sailing conditions had remained good, although the wind direction kept us close-hauled and made our progress slow and sailing somewhat difficult and uncomfortable. However, everything aboard ship was functioning smoothly. With the wind now coming from even further north and with all systems functioning well so far, I made the decision to forgo the stop at Ofu and instead to fall off and set a new course toward Christmas Island.

On the new course, with our increased speed, I expected to hail Christmas in two weeks. This meant that for the next week, I would have the option of turning back to Samoa should any serious problems arise. After that we would have passed the point-of-no-return where it would be shorter to go on than to turn back.

As we fell off, our speed predictably increased, and sailing became more comfortable. Sadie and I quickly settled into our daily sailing routine. Although she was not dogging my footsteps, she liked to be where she could see me. If I was forward, she'd come forward too and find a corner where she could sit and watch from a distance. Therefore, anytime I missed seeing her for awhile, I would go looking, often finding her fast asleep, curled up near the radio shelf in a cubby hole just the right size for her to fit into.

Sadie was great company during what would otherwise have been lonely days stretching into lonely weeks at sea. There is

Figure 6   **Sadie meets a parrot fish at the base of the main mast.**

great solitude at sea, and I think some of the single-handed
sailors that I have met have become a little mad by the isolation
of being alone at sea too long. It is most unusual to see anything
at all in the blue water of mid ocean. The total number of ship
sightings after a day or more at sea, probably average one ship
in two weeks. More often than not, after departing one port I
would see no other ship until arrival in the next port.

I found airplane sightings even more rare than ship sightings,
although jet contrails frequently mark air lanes near busy
airports ashore, and it is rumored inexperienced sailors have
used contrails to find Hawaii. Until this trip, the only low-level
flight I ever saw offshore was a military helicopter that came out
to investigate as we sailed by Johnston Atoll during the Vietnam
War. We must have appeared on the long distance radar
although we were more than a hundred miles from the forbidden
waters around the atoll.

20

Although land birds were frequently the first sign of approaching an island still out of sight over the horizon, the mid ocean is more barren than most deserts. While not quite as sparse as ships and planes at sea, sea life is not as common as one might expect. Trolling lines were run out from the aft rail of *Haleakala* on almost every voyage, but the only fish we caught trolling were in the shallow waters around islands or over the continental shelf.

Sea Life & Life at Sea

The relatively abundant sea life was probably the most unusual part of this particular voyage. Almost every day I saw birds fishing on small schools of fish even though we were sailing in deep water, not passing near or approaching any islands after moving beyond Ta'u. We saw several schools of porpoises roaming the high seas and even a land bird, seemingly lost in the deep ocean hundreds of miles from shore. Many times Sadie would be the first to spot life in the sea.

A few porpoises would find us once or twice on almost every voyage to swim along with the boat for an hour or two before moving off ahead of us. But porpoises, too, were more common near shore. I remembered the time when *Haleakala* was anchored off of Christmas Island a couple of years before, and hundreds and hundreds of porpoises swam by churning up the water between the boat and shore. A few days later another school of two dozen porpoises escorted us into Christmas Lagoon.

In the early evening of our fourth day out, while I sat on deck leaning against the cabin back writing in the log, I noticed Sadie staring intently into the water. I turned to see where she was looking and saw two dolphins swimming along in synchronization with the boat. I put down the log, and we watched in fascination as the dolphins swam around and around the boat. Although we were traveling between seven and eight knots at the time, the dolphins had no difficulty swimming circles around us. After a while they seemed to tire of the game and disappeared.

I settled back and was just adding the dolphin sighting to the log when the ocean around us became alive, filled with dolphins. The first two must have gone to get their friends and relatives. These were spinner dolphins, and they were putting on a show! Everywhere I looked there were leaping, spinning dolphins. Individuals, groups of two, three, even four or five at a time would jump and spin for us.

I had never before seen spinning dolphins in their natural habitat. They gave a spectacular performance. Free, in their native environment they seemed to be bursting with joy. Their show, just for Sadie and me, continued into the sunset, and I had to finish that day's log below in the cabin light.

Over the next couple of days the wind kept shifting uncharacteristically further to the north. To maintain our course and speed, I had to compensate by sheeting in the sails tighter and tighter. As the wind shifted, it also freshened, and the signs of an impending storm appeared. The cloud cover increased, and the sky grew darker and darker. I knew we were in for some heavy weather, which threatened to be more intense than the squalls being forecast for our area of the south equatorial Pacific Ocean. Sadie began staying below most of the time as the storm approached.

The wind speed increased, and I started reducing the sail area by reefing the mainsail and mizzen in stages until both were in the second reef. The working jib was performing well and not yet overpowered, so I left it in place on the forestay. In this configuration, we sailed through three more days of moderately heavy weather. The storm brought downpours and gusts over 30 knots, and the constant tossing by the wind and waves made sailing exhausting.

I was feeling the strain of sailing in bad weather as we began the fourth stormy day. I was getting less than an hour of sleep at a time, in short cat naps between storm watches. By the end of the fourth full day of heavy weather sailing, the average wind conditions had gotten up to the previous gust speeds and the gusts were now over 40 knots. I decided to reduce sail even further to a minimum configuration so that I could get more needed rest. I would drop the working jib[10] from the dual forestay, raise the storm jib on the intermediate forestay, drop the main, and take another reef in the mizzen. This would

---

[10]Rephrased in English, I would replace the moderately large sails with smaller ones and thereby re-configure the boat to be able to handle even more severe winds.

greatly reduce the speed of the boat and the associated motion which, in turn, would allow me to relax a bit and get some sleep.

It was early evening as I went on deck to put the sails in the new configuration. As always, while out of the cabin I wore my harness and clipped on to the standing rigging in the subconscious habit I had developed. I dropped the main and tied it to the boom with several gaskets, dropped the working jib and lashed it to the railing, hoisted the storm jib on the intermediate forestay, and finally pulled the mizzen into the last reef.

It was hard, exhausting work struggling alone with the large sails in a choppy sea. It was just beginning to get dark when I finished. I returned to the cabin, made a fresh pot of coffee, and sat down to drink a cup and enter the sail change in the log. As I was writing, I noticed the storm was no longer as strong as it had been when I first went out on deck to reduce the sail area. In a momentary lull I looked up from the chart table and could see a most magnificent sight.

On my left a wall of black clouds rose from the sea as far up as I could see. On the right was a clear sky with shining stars. Apparently we had just sailed right out from under the storm clouds. Even as tired as I was, I went out on deck to get a better view of this spectacular sight, to stare in awe at this wonder of nature. The great black wall of boiling clouds stretched out for several miles on the left while ahead and to the right the air was clear. Only one big black cloud remained hovering in our path half a mile ahead. It certainly would be easy to steer clear of the one cloud.

So, just after I had finished reefing for more heavy weather we were beyond it. I briefly considered going to work and putting all the sails back up. But my fatigue and the thought of sleep easily won out over any thought of sail change. So, now ghosting along with only the storm jib and mizzen in third reef providing power, I went below and instantly fell into a deep slumber. It was the best undisturbed sleep I had on the voyage.

The next morning I awoke refreshed to watch the dawn before beginning my morning ritual. The sun rose in a clear sky dotted with small fluffy clouds. This particular cloud formation is quite common where the warm tropic air picks up moisture flowing over the flat expanse of equally warm ocean. The friction of the atmosphere against the sea seems to cause it to tumble in a somersaulting motion, taking some of the moisture laden air up from the surface to the chill of the higher altitudes causing the dot, dot, dot clouds.[11]

Sadie and I were comfortable and safe aboard the spacious *Haleakala.* When I was designing her I had considered the conflicting size requirements of a ship design. More size usually means more safety and certainly more comfort but it also compounds the difficulties of sailing, particularly solo sailing.

---

[11]Feedback from a meteorologist indicates that this sailor's explanation, although fanciful and similar to the characteristics of a boundary turbulence layer, may be more of a story than an explanation. To quote John Flanigan:

"I've never heard that explanation for fair weather cumulus. These clouds are also common over land. They are a feature of relatively stable air with moderate moisture content. Since there is no orographic effect at sea, and little of the differential heating typical of continental land masses, these harbingers of fair weather are more common over water."

Having sailed in the typically cramped living space aboard other vessels, I decided on the largest design that I felt was able to be solo-sailed. The large size of *Haleakala* provided considerable privacy and comfort even with a full crew of ten aboard, while still being manageable, although difficult to sail alone.

There was enough room aboard that frequently many conversations were occurring at the same time. The cabin top served as a twenty foot square sun deck for lounging and sunbathing. The forward deck, ahead of the cabin portlights (windows) was made in the form of a large bench which sat six to eight people comfortably. The aft cockpit area had two lounging areas, each the size of a double bed. The main salon had held 27 people during one party aboard. The galley area was made more narrow than the main salon area, partly to avoid injuries while cooking in a rough sea. However, it frequently had three or four people in it at the same time. Further below the main salon were the staterooms where off duty crew lounged, read, and had more private conversations. Last, but not least to mention, was the forward net. The net was constructed of two inch wide nylon webbing interlaced to provide comfortable support and felt much like a large hammock. Many nights were spent by crew sleeping on the net while we were underway. It was also delightful to watch the sea rolling under the boat while lying on the net.

Large size also presents the obvious associated sailing difficulties such as large sails, that are difficult to handle, and, therefore, require conservative deployment when shorthanded. However, the most serious problem I faced was less obvious, namely maintaining a personal awareness of the total vessel. Even with a crew, the large size, with her multiple compartments on several levels, made it difficult to stay aware of all of the myriad things that could go wrong. I faithfully went through a morning ritual to help ensure that nothing needing attention was missed because *Haleakala* was short handed.

As usual, I began my morning ritual with a complete inspection tour of the ship above and below decks. It seems most wear and tear occurs at night. Maybe the sailing weather is more severe at night or maybe the poorer visibility allows problems to go undetected until daylight. The large size of the vessel also made it easy to overlook problems unless one went looking for them. In any case, I found morning inspection tours to be the most valuable form of preventive maintenance.

I opened hatches to check for bilge water and inspected the rigging for signs of abnormal wear and potential failure. I paid particular attention to the standing rigging looking for small cracks, knowing how stainless steel work-hardens under stress causing hairline cracks to appear overnight. I checked the running rigging for chafe, the blocks and shackles for undue wear.

Then I was ready to put on full sail while also checking each sail for fatigue and seam failure. This morning I took extra time and care to inspect the sails as they were deployed; the stress of several days of heavy weather sailing could take its toll on sails. Starting with the mainsail, I shook the reefs out[12] one set at a time and inspected the material as I hoisted it in stages to the

---

[12]Briefly, sails are made effectively smaller by reefing, which consists of lowering the sail part way, bunching the excess material into a small roll, and putting heavy cords around the roll. The sail is then made larger again by untying these cords and pulling the now larger sail, back up into place on the mast.

masthead. Next I dropped the storm jib and began raising the working jib. While hoisting and inspecting it I noticed a worn spot about two feet long with a small tear in the middle. Now my day's work was cut out for me; today I would be making sail repairs.

Sailing with the jib so tightly sheeted had caused it to rub on the upper spreader. Continued chafing had worn through the spreader boot eventually allowing the sail to rub on the now exposed metal at the end of the spreader.

I considered repairing both the sail and the spreader boot. With two spare boots in ship's stores I could have replaced one using the bosun's chair to go aloft. I had a block and tackle already rigged to the chair to ascend the mast, but it is laborious and dangerous to go aloft while at sea and especially so when solo sailing. Single-handing also meant that I would have to haul myself aloft without the use of the winches which I would normally have used with another crewman aboard. Assessing the situation, I decided not to go up. I would repair the sail with extra reinforcement and consider replacing the spreader boot later, and then only if the extra reinforcement wore through.[13]

As the storm jib was still hanked on to the intermediate forestay, I raised this small sail again even though I could use more foresail area. I had not yet reviewed the morning weather forecast, but the scattered little clouds indicated the moderate trade winds should continue throughout the day with no pending

---

[13]This would be unlikely unless it became necessary to again sail hard on the weather. If the wind shifted more northerly the options would be to fall-off further or to tack, both would be giving ground to prevent further sail damage.

heavy weather. I briefly thought about hoisting the Genoa jib instead of leaving only the small storm jib as the headsail. It was readily available, already hanked on one of the forestay, and lashed to the net and rail every couple of feet to keep it from flying free. It was a full overlap Genoa that would have produced significant additional speed. But I had planned only to use it in extremely light air, and the air was now a little too fresh to make me comfortable using it. I dismissed the idea and kept the mizzen reefed to balance the small storm jib and prepared to repair and reinforce the working jib.

Starting at the head, I unhanked enough of the sail to get the chafed spot below through the open overhead hatch. I then drew the sail through the hatch onto the main salon table. Next I broke out the sewing machine and started the engine for power. With the large alternator on the main engine, I had enough electric power[14] to run not only the sewing machine, but all of the other appliances aboard, simultaneously.

From early morning until mid afternoon I worked on the sail with the sewing machine where possible, and by hand using a sailor's palm when the thickness and/or bulk of the sailcloth was beyond the sewing machine capacity. By four o'clock the work was finished. The working jib was again run up the forestay. By now the point of sail was more off the weather than before the storm, meaning the jib was not as tightly sheeted in, so it no longer chafed on the spreader. Still I planned to keep an eye on

---

[14]The 120 Volt 60 cycle AC alternator was rated at 7.5 KW continuously and would support a 20% overload, intermittently.

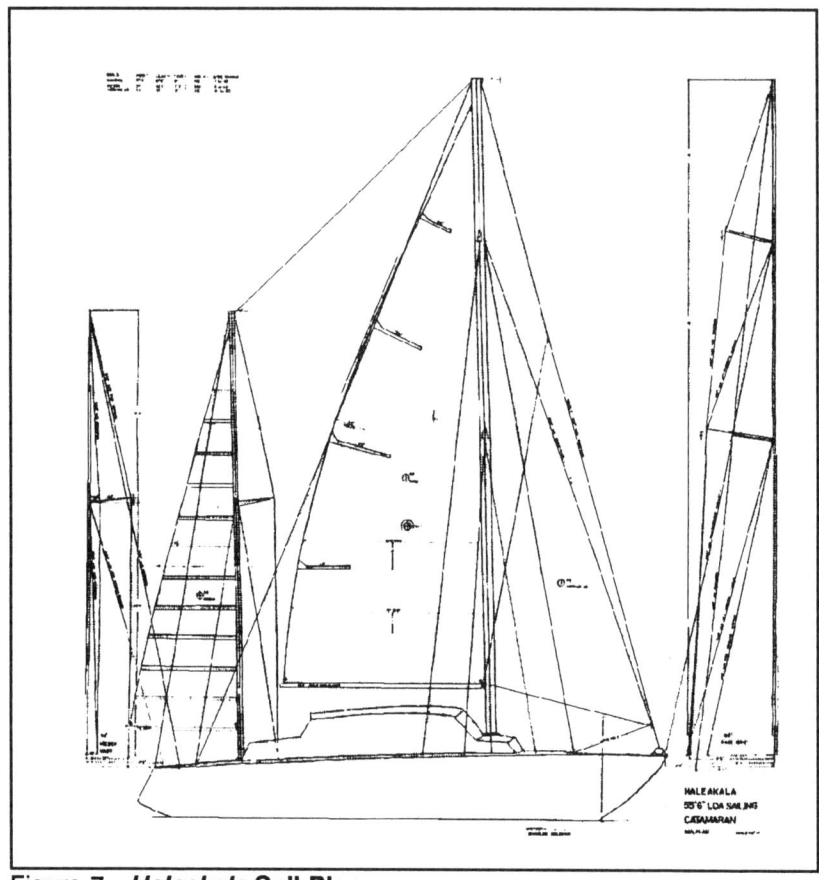

Figure 7   *Haleakala* **Sail Plan.**

the exposed spreader tip and the sail chafe area.[15]

Nearing the equator the sunsets seemed to become progressively more spectacular. On Good Friday, Sadie and I enjoyed what was expected to be our last supper in the South

---

[15]Should the extra layers of reinforcement on the sail begin to wear through, I would fall-off, tack, or then face the decision to either continue to repair the sail with more reinforcement and/or to go aloft to install a new spreader boot.

Pacific before crossing the equator. As usual of late, we both went out on deck after dinner to watch yet another magnificent sunset. I doubt that Sadie could appreciate the beauty of the sunset, but she sat quietly beside me as I watched the vivid color of the sky as the sun approached the horizon. The clouds were streaked in layers of cool blue, bright orange, and fiery red, against dark purple clouds at the horizon. The sky above the setting sun was a light blue deepening overhead until it was a deep blue-black in the east.

I watched in silent admiration as we sat on the aft deck until the sun had set and all of the color had faded from the sky. Everything was peaceful and quiet as we later settled into an uninterrupted night's sleep with no premonition of dire events that tomorrow would bring.

Nothing Amiss

I woke to a beautiful dawn as we approached within thirty miles of the equator. The day began with the usual routine. My own experience supports the old saw that sailing is "hours of boredom punctuated by moments of sheer terror." But there is always plenty to do to occupy those boring hours. The dot, dot, dot of tropical clouds still spread across the horizon. My morning inspection revealed nothing amiss. All bilges were dry and no signs of impending failure could be seen anywhere in the rigging. I noted the weather and ship's condition in the log. Everything looked shipshape as I prepared for my morning shower and breakfast.

I looked forward to a salt water shower every morning unless it was raining hard enough to enjoy a fresh water shower. Whenever there was a steady downpour, fresh water was available at the base of the mainmast. The mast stood taller than a seven story building[16] and the sails each had the proper area to match the size of the mast. Much rain was collected by the large area of the sail, to run down the windward side and cascade off the boom at the gooseneck. First I had to wait long enough to let the rain wash off the salt spray from the sail. Then the first batch of clean rain water was used to top off the water tanks if they were at all low, and finally, I would luxuriate in a refreshing shower of soft rainwater. I would take a rain water shower whenever possible. The torrent of fresh water was so refreshing I would take a rain water shower even in the middle of the night with a chill in the air.

Although rainwater makes the best shower, saltwater is wonderful when you are hot and sticky and in need of a bath, or even as a wake-up refresher. I stripped, except for safety harness, lathered-up with dish detergent, scrubbed, and doused myself with buckets of fresh seawater until all the detergent was flushed away.

Fresh from the salt water shower, I made my breakfast of canned ham and fresh fried eggs, gave Sadie some dry cat food,

---

[16]Once a sailmaker friend came to visit while *Haleakala* was tied to a transient dock in a California marina. He apparently had some difficulty locating the vessel because as he came aboard he remarked, "*Haleakala* has the second tallest mast in this marina." Looking around at the other nearby vessels and not immediately spotting any taller rig, I had to ask which vessel had the tallest mast. He replied, "*Haleakala* has that one too!"

which she loved,[17] and sat at the chart table to eat and listen to the radio. During breakfast, I usually reviewed my progress from the previous day and considered changes in sailing tactics. Since course changes would depend on the weather, I listened for weather forecasts from Honolulu, and then to the Breakfast Club ham radio net for information about sailing conditions in the Pacific Basin.

I charted the current position of *Haleakala*, projected that we would cross the Equator just before noon, and weighed the advisability of altering course. This daily reevaluation of course and direction was more important than sticking to the original sail plan which is based on accumulated weather data from the sailing charts for the route and time the passage is planned. These accumulated weather synopsis charts give the general wind and current patterns by the season of the year and cover all of the ocean routes of the world. However, once sailing in an area, the actual weather and currents, of course, must override any statistical data summarized on the charts.[18]

---

[17]At first Sadie was fed canned tuna cat food fresh from the cannery in Pago Pago Harbor. After a steady diet of tuna, she apparently "overdosed" because she refused to eat any more tuna, switching instead to the imported dry cat food.

[18]Over the years, rules-of-thumb have been developed for sailing the world's ocean passages. While valuable to know, this sailing lore cannot be followed to the letter. For example, traditional sailor wisdom says easting is "money in the bank" for the voyage between Samoa and Hawaii in either direction. Following this advise, I had maintained easting on the trip down from Christmas Island to Samoa. Unfortunately, the day before we hailed Samoa the wind changed direction by nearly 180 degrees, a most unusual direction for Samoa. So, instead of an easy downwind sail, we spent the last day of the trip motoring directly to weather.

The heavy weather we had been through was now long behind us and had been replaced by beautiful weather. Moderate trade winds filled the sails as *Haleakala* continued to make good progress. Stormy weather is rare near the equator, and sailors generally expect doldrums instead of storms in the latitudes just to the north of the equator. In the past I had found the monotony of these doldrums to be harder on crew than sailing in moderately heavy weather. Lying around with nothing to do, basking in the sunshine with sails slapping may sound ideal, but being stalled in the ocean without making progress toward port definitely raises tempers. Storms may be exhausting but there is little time to think about petty problems while working hard to combat the weather.

Knowledge of local weather conditions and current predictions is crucial to safe sailing, and reliable weather information is available on shortwave radio from a number of stations. WWVH in Hawaii provides a synopsis and forecast of the Pacific Ocean weather in addition to accurate time signals for navigation, while WWV in Boulder, Colorado, simultaneously provides the same time signals but with the Atlantic Ocean forecasts. To supplement WWVH, I had made a list of about 20 other radio weather sources with the frequencies, times of broadcast, and geographic area covered by the information broadcast by each station. FAX weather data is also broadcast on short wave radio, and I had a FAX schedule, although I did not yet have a FAX machine.[19]

I found the general weather information on WWVH to be fairly accurate but on a rather coarse geographic scale. Even though the coverage area is large, the information that was broadcast kept me well informed on the location and extent of severe weather conditions. While at sea I copied into the ship's log, the latitude and longitude of all cyclones as well as the location of the major highs and lows. If WWVH reception was poor, or if I just wanted more information for my own particular area, I would tune in one or more of the other more local weather stations on my list. This gathering of weather data was an important part of my morning activities, and I persisted until I felt I understood the forecast with sufficient detail and accuracy. I then logged the detailed weather conditions and sea state for both my present location and destination—the Central Pacific and the waters off the Hawaiian Islands.

This morning no storms were expected in either of these areas for the next 48 hours. The nearest heavy weather, the storm I had sailed through, was well behind me and at least 200 miles away. There were some small rain clouds about, but I expected little more than dampened decks should I sail beneath one. However, at my destination, Hawaii, small craft advisories were in effect from increasing north northwest winds. This is an unusual wind direction for Hawaii, and I did not expect it to

---

[19]I was considering getting a FAX machine on arrival in Honolulu, because of the favorable comments from sailors who owned them. A FAX receiver could have been connected to the computer I had aboard, so that the computer's dot-matrix printer could also have been used to print the FAX.

continue long enough still to be a problem on my arrival in Honolulu.

The local winds were still from the northeast although prevailing southeast trade winds are normally to be expected in our present area south of the equator. There is a general expectation of a shift to light east winds or doldrums when crossing north of the equator. This pattern is most common just north of the equator but can range further to the north or conversely, be found further south even in the southern hemisphere.

Considering the northerly wind direction, the fact that all systems aboard *Haleakala* were functioning well, and the fact that we did not require a stop at Christmas Island, I decided to fall off[20] even more. This would allow us to gain speed toward Hawaii rather than continue a course hard on the weather which was required in order to maintain enough easting to lay in to Christmas Island. If a stop at Christmas should later become necessary, I could always tack back or motor to weather to fetch the island.

My new course was more to the west of Christmas and east of Palmyra Island. This would keep me well to the east of the rhumb line to Hawaii but further to the west than originally planned. I entered the new course into the auto pilot and then noted the change and reasoning in the log. The course change consideration was the last step of this morning's ritual. Now I could get on with my daily activities.

---

[20]To fall off means to turn further away from the direction that the wind is blowing from so that the sails fill better and the sea pounding is reduced.

I busied myself with odd jobs, one of which was checking the batteries of all flashlights, strobes, and radios and replacing any having a low voltage.[21] Before every voyage, I always put new batteries in the strobes and flashlights regardless of how long the old batteries had been in service. I also checked the voltage of all new batteries before I put them in any safety gear to make sure they had not discharged before being used. The moist salty air of the tropics can discharge a battery even while it is sitting on the shelf. I also stored batteries in a watertight plastic bag in the refrigerator, when it was running, to extend their shelf life.

The day had remained as predicted. The sky was nearly clear from horizon to horizon except for the little clouds dotting the tropical sky, occasionally making small patches of rain. Sadie and I were relaxing after lunch, she dozing on the pilot berth and I working at the chart table. I was studying the charts of the Hawaiian Island group, considering course changes I might make if the wind did not soon veer back to the more normal direction. The course calculations showed that we had crossed the equator just an hour before noon, and were back in the northern hemisphere for the first time in several years.

It was excellent sailing weather, and *Haleakala* was making a bit under eight knots in the moderate winds. Now seemed a good time to check provisions. We had been underway for two weeks and continuing at the current speed, we would be in Honolulu in less than two more weeks. This meant that there

---

[21]During this time I evidently put a battery in my pocket because I found it there many hours later, heavily corroded by salt water.

should be at least half of the provisions remaining for the rest of the trip.

Less than 55 gallons of diesel fuel had been used and more than 140 gallons remained in the main tanks with an additional 60 gallons in reserve in plastic fuel cans.

Over 30 gallons of water had been used with 90 gallons remaining in the main water tanks plus an additional 30 gallons in water bottles. That should be plenty even without any rain water refills.

Food stores were, in a word, excessive. The cases and cases of canned food plus the dry food stores would last Sadie and me a number of months. I had no worries about provisions.

Bang!

I was shaken out of my thoughts about provisions by a tremendous bang! A ripping, crunching noise followed as *Haleakala* shuddered in her tracks. I can still vividly recall the heart-stopping reverberation of the noise of the big bang, and the memory of it still brings chills to my spine. I jumped up at the first sound, and my immediate thought was I had struck something in the water. But striking a reef seemed impossible. A glance at the charts in front of me showed the nearest land was Christmas Island about 400 miles away.

There had been nothing on the horizon, and there was nothing I could see now. Even on watch a sailor does not keep his eyes glued to the sea but scans the horizon from time to time to keep aware of what is going on. I had a clear view all around the boat from my seat at the chart table, and nothing unusual was in sight in any direction.

I immediately rushed out on deck and, keeping myself clipped on, went around the boat to look for damage. The sound had seemed to come from the port side, so I started my search at the stern on the port side, leaning over the rail to see if there were any holes or cracks in the outer hull. I searched all the way forward to the bow without finding anything wrong. I crossed the foredeck, went up to the starboard bow and continued the search back along the starboard side. Working my way back to the stern, I still found nothing wrong. I decided to make a more careful, detailed inspection.[22]

Finding no damage on the outboard hulls, I started examining the bilges, again first on the port side, because that was where the sound had seemed to originate. I lifted the floor boards in the port amidship stateroom and found the bilge to be dry. I then moved to the port head and then the port aft stateroom, also finding the bilges dry.

With no apparent leaks below, I went out on deck again and, still taking care to remain clipped on with my safety line, I opened the hatch to the port rudder compartment finding it too was dry. I closed it and again dogged it tight. (All hatches were kept tightly dogged when at sea.)

Going forward to the port bow I opened the hatch to the forward bow compartment, which contained two of the four main water tanks and where I stowed mooring lines, spare anchors,

---

[22]The construction drawing of the vessel is reproduced as Figure 8 so that the reader can follow the damage assessment scenario.

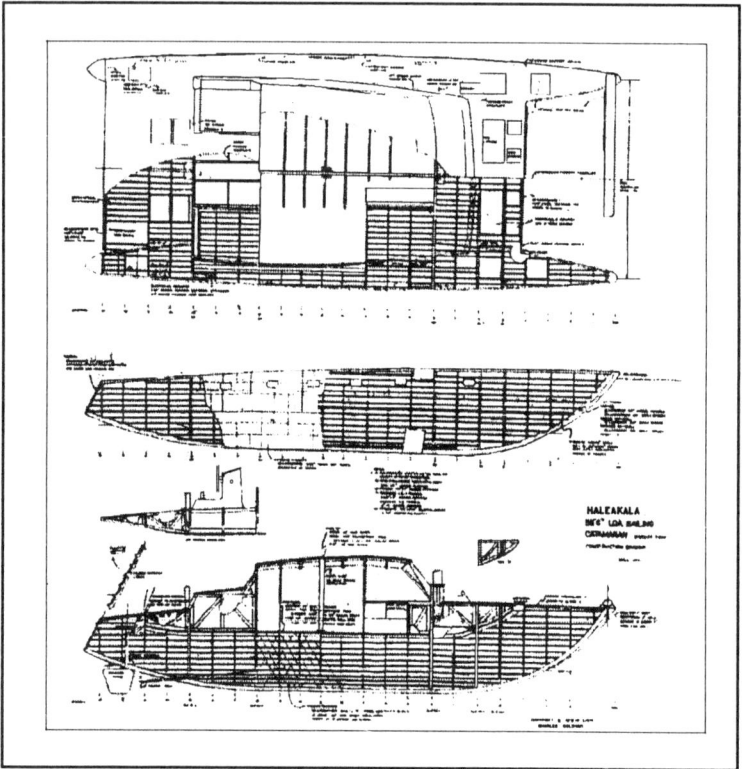

Figure 8 **The Construction Drawing of *Haleakala*.**

and electrical wire. This compartment was also dry.

The last remaining hatch on the port side was access to the port forward stateroom. A 45 pound Danforth anchor, attached to 300 feet of 5/8 inch line, was mounted there within easy reach. This stateroom was being used for the stowage of carpentry tools and assorted pieces of teak.

I opened the hatch and looked down into the compartment. I could see right through the hull to the light blue water of the ocean!

There was a hole[23] in *Haleakala*!

Although any breach in a hull is an extremely serious problem at sea, I thought that *Haleakala* was not in immediate catastrophic danger because of the watertight bulkhead[24] separating the punctured compartment with the hole from the main salon and the rest of the boat.

From the location and appearance of the hole, I thought I must have hit a log in the water. I stood up and looked aft to see if there was anything floating behind the boat. Nothing was visible in the water behind the boat all of the way to the horizon.[25]

---

[23]The hole was about the size of a man's head and six inches below the water line on the inboard side of the port bow directly below the leading edge of the wing bridge.

[24]I had designed *Haleakala* with three watertight bulkheads athwart-ship and two watertight partitions running fore-and-aft for a total of six watertight compartments, three in each of the two hulls. The first watertight bulkhead was the collision bulkhead required by the Coast Guard for all passenger vessels, forming a water tight compartment in each bow. Aft of the collision bulkhead and forward of the main mast were two staterooms, one on the port side and one on the starboard side. These were separated from each other by a watertight partition and from the cabin salon by the main mast bulkhead forming the second pair of watertight compartments aft of the bow. Aft of this bulkhead on each side were two staterooms separated by a full head. Finally the last watertight bulkhead partitioned the aft staterooms from the two separate watertight rudder compartments.

[25]Although I saw nothing in the water at that moment, enough time had passed since the collision for such an object to have passed well out of sight behind the boat. It had to have been low in the water and could have been underneath the wing as I was going forward inspecting the outboard hull. By the time I had examined both outboard hulls and returned to the stern it must already have passed out of sight.

My first concern was to stop the water flowing into the compartment and to make temporary repairs as rapidly as possible. Since the sound of the impact had come from the port side and the damage I now found was also on the port side, it did not seem reasonable to spend much more time now in search of other damage on the starboard side. Therefore, taking only a very fast peek in the remaining hatches, and finding no additional damage on the starboard side, I hurried aft to the cockpit.

Stepping to the helm, I disengaged the auto pilot, brought the boat up across the weather until the jib was backwinded, set the helm brake to hold *Haleakala* hove-to under sail, and then went forward and dropped the main. This maneuver stopped all further pounding into the sea and partially sheltered the hole from the rush of the incoming water.

As I dropped the main I realized now was the time to activate the EPIRB[26]. In mid ocean, taking on water through a breached hull was serious enough to warrant having the EPIRB transmitting; it was not clear just how serious the damage was nor when I would be able to get underway again. My life was clearly in danger. Waiting too long to call for help would greatly reduce our chances of survival. Response to an active EPIRB is ordinarily slow, and I could always turn it off later if I were able to make repairs and get underway without help. I

---

[26]EPIRB stands for Emergency Position Indicating Radio Beacon. It is an emergency radio that must be carried aboard all commercial ships, licensed aircraft, and by vessels engaged in sanctioned offshore racing. An EPIRB is also recommended, but not required, equipment for all vessels engaged in offshore passages. In an emergency it can be used to transmit a signal by which the vessel's location can be determined.

knew it was better to turn on the EPIRB while I was able to do so rather than to wait until it was too late.

The EPIRB was mounted in a holder by the chart table where it could be readily accessed and deployed in an emergency. I stepped below, pulled open the switch cover, turned the EPIRB on, and replaced the water tight cover.

With the EPIRB activated, I went out on deck to start the engine. I needed the engine to pump out the water from the bilge and to supply the electric power for making repairs. From the first look at the hole, it was clear that it was too large for the bilge pump to make headway until there was a patch in place. However, it would do no harm to have it already pumping, and it would become increasingly effective as progress was made toward plugging the hole.

I went below to activate the 120 Volt AC invertor and to turn on the single circuit breaker supplying the port forward stateroom. There was no fear of a short circuit at that time because the AC outlets and wiring were mounted as high on the bulkheads as possible. This meant there could be no 120 Volt short circuit unless the hull filled completely with water, and that looked improbable from the first inspection.

Gathering up a hammer, a box of ringed boat nails, the electric saber saw, and my snorkel and mask from the hook by the door, I rushed back. Climbing down the hatch I proceeded to examine the full extent of the collision damage. *Haleakala* was built using the latest techniques of light-weight, high-strength multi-hull construction.[27] The ribs and stringers held the skin in the designed curve so that much of the structural strength came from the skin rather than from the ribs. Although this "skin stressed" structure was designed to be very strong, it had not been able to withstand this impact without extensive damage.

Haleakala had obviously struck with tremendous force against something nearly immovable in the water.[28] At the point of impact, the entire plywood frame that had been there as well as all of the stringers above and below it were destroyed. Broken splinters and chips floated on the water flooding the bilge. The impact had been hard enough to shatter the wood of the hull.

Not only were all nine plies of the hull delaminated, but for a two-foot diameter around the hole all that remained were limp splinters of wood fiber rather than the more expected type of damage consisting of separated, but intact, plywood layers.

At the center of the damage was an eight to ten inch diameter hole bordered by the shattered wood. The next foot

---

[27]*Haleakala* was designed according to Coast Guard standards and specifications for passenger vessels. In addition, heavier scantlings than were required, in fact those appropriate for a 62 foot catamaran, were used to provide an additional safety factor for ocean cruising.

The construction details included 4-1/2" wide frames made of 3/4" marine plywood spaced 28 inches apart. 7/8" by 1-1/4" stringers were spaced every six inches running the full length of the ship. The outer hull was made of three layers of diagonally staggered 5/32" three-ply marine plywood molded over the stringers.

[28]The impact point was in a watertight compartment; the forward stateroom was made watertight by the bulkheads that formed the ends of the staterooms. The hole was midway aft of the collision bulkhead and forward of the main mast bulkhead and six inches below the water line.

radiating outward was progressively, pulp, shredded wood fibers, and finally delaminated plies. The following foot appeared to have progressively more sound plywood continuing outward until the bulkhead strength came into play preventing further damage.

With this compartment flooded, the boat would still float in acceptable trim. In fact, *Haleakala* could even sail at diminished, but quite adequate speed, with both forward compartments flooded. Had the impact been ahead of the collision bulkhead, it would have resulted in even less of a problem because *Haleakala* should be able to sail with both bows crushed and flooded. It thus appeared I might repair this damage and get underway again without outside help.

To plug the hole, a patch had to be nailed in place from inside the boat, and only then could the compartment be pumped as dry as possible.

I picked up one of the floorboards floating about and cut it with the saber saw into a patch that would fit between the remaining frames and cover the hole. Using a handful of the special holding boat nails, I first partially hammered them in around the edges of the patch. With the nails partially in and spaced around the patch, and with the water continuing to rise in the compartment, I had to use the mask and snorkel to hold the patch in place under water while I nailed it to the hull. Because of the hull curvature, the flat patch did not fit flush to the hull. Therefore, after the first patch was in place, I planned to cut a second, larger, patch to go over the first in order to provide the extended coverage needed for a better water seal.

I climbed out of the compartment and went aft, again checking inside all of the hatches. Even though I assumed the single hole on the port side was the only damage, I continued to look for possible additional problems. I didn't want to overlook any leaks elsewhere. With the first patch stemming some of the water flow, I now could take the time for a more complete damage assessment. Climbing down inside each hatch to lift all of the compartment floorboards, I was relieved to find each bilge completely dry. Now, I could return forward to install the second patch.

I decided to make an overlay patch twice as large as the initial patch, extending the coverage all around the hole. I hoped an additional patch would stop the inflow of the sea water. There were still two more floorboards floating in the compartment but both were too small to use for the second patch. I climbed out to get a larger piece of plywood from the supply stored in the starboard forward stateroom. I marked it to size, cut it to shape, and nailed it over top of the first patch. As I worked under water with the snorkel and mask I could tell the first patch had significantly reduced but not stopped the water flowing into the compartment.

When the second patch was securely in place, it appeared to work so well in reducing the inflow of water I felt confident I would be able to completely seal any remaining leak with the underwater epoxy I carried aboard. I was elated at the successful repair work I had been able to accomplish and was looking forward to a break.[29]

Flooding Amidship

I had noticed a steady rise in the level of the water in the compartment while I was working. This was more of a subconscious awareness while I was busy making repairs, rather than a conscious concern. I had not yet taken the time to fully consider the ramifications of the rising water level while I worked, but it was now beginning to worry me. As I climbed out of the hatch, what concerned me most was that there might be some amidship flooding I had not found on my initial inspections. I noticed the port bow was deeper in the water than I would have expected with just the one forward stateroom flooded. I took a quick peek in the bow compartment just to make sure this compartment, ahead of the collision bulkhead, had not also been damaged. It was still dry.

I worried more about the list of the boat as I checked the setting of the bilge pump valves to make sure the flooded compartment was indeed being drained. It occurred to me to check the rudder compartments more thoroughly. I had not

---

[29]Time had seemed to flash by while I had been working frantically, and although it seemed mere minutes, later review of all that happened indicates that it must have been a couple of hours from when I first heard the bang until the second patch was in place.

climbed down inside them before because they had no floor boards concealing the bilge. However, I wanted to be certain there was no water hidden beneath the spare fuel cans stored there. I found them to be bone dry.

By now the list to port really became the focus of my attention and concern. It had not increased by any noticeable amount in the few minutes since I had finished the overlay patch but it was too much of a list to accept as reasonable under the circumstances. I had more checking to do and possibly more repairs to make.

As I entered the cabin I was worried that there could be as yet unnoticed additional damage and flooding on the starboard side which would have lowered the boat into the water. This, in turn, would have exaggerated the forward pitch, increasing the flooding of the port forward compartment, and causing the resultant list. I had not thoroughly checked the central compartments before I made the hole repair because all indications had been that the damage was confined to the port forward stateroom.

I went down the aft companionway ladder and started my inspection in the starboard aft stateroom. As rapidly as I could, I lifted all of the floorboards, working forward from the aft stateroom through the head to the amidship stateroom. I found all the starboard bilges were dry. If there was additional damage and flooding, it would also have to be on the port side. I headed across the main cabin down to the port amidship stateroom and started checking under the floorboards. I was horrified to find several inches of water in the bilge.

I definitely had flooding amidship!

When I traced the source of the bilge water I found it was coming from the forward end of the compartment, flowing around the "watertight" main bulkhead, running down and back along the inside of the inboard hull, and spilling into the bilge.

At that moment it became more clear to me what must have been the chain of events: A massive, still unidentified, floating object holed *Haleakala* in the port forward compartment. But, the hole was only the initial impact point. That long crunching sound immediately following the bang was the sound of the object ripping along the entire length of the hull, tearing free the skin, and gashing the entire inboard side of the hull. This would be similar to the assumed damage to the Titanic attributed to the iceberg which broke the watertight integrity of the entire hull.

I could not verify my conclusions about the full extent of the damage without seeing the outside surface of the port hull. To do this, I would have to get into the sea, swim between the hulls, and then dive down and examine the outside surface of the inboard hull aft of the impact point. Nevertheless, even without physical inspection, the internal leakage convinced me that the hull was cracked for some distance back from the impact point and possibly beyond the last bulkhead at the back of the boat.

While I had been working on plugging the hole, the boat was listing further to port with the bow pitched down. As the flooding continued through the cracked side and around the bulkhead, the angle of list increased, making the water rise higher in the forward stateroom further increasing the flow aft around the bulkhead.

When I built *Haleakala* I had installed flotation to counter this problem of amidship flooding including the flooding of an additional forward compartment on the same side.[30] Now I would be forced to test the secondary stability calculations.

Although the ports were already dogged shut, I went along on both sides to check and to tighten the dogs down on their rubber gaskets as hard as I could by hand.

It was apparent that what had been a clear EPIRB emergency had suddenly become a Mayday disaster. I now faced the very real possibility of losing *Haleakala*! Obviously there was more serious damage than I had originally realized. In addition to the EPIRB, it was now time to broadcast a Mayday! With this much damage my chances of getting underway without help were nearly nil. I had to consider that *Haleakala* might founder, leaving me in grave and immediate danger, alone in the middle of the ocean.

---

[30]To counterbalance the resultant list, a total of (negative) 10,000 pounds of flotation was built into the bulkheads and wing (the structure between the two hulls of a catamaran.) This, as well as the flotation remaining in the bow and stern compartments, should stabilize *Haleakala* with about a 20 degree list to port depending on the sea state. At this angle, although the ports would be awash, further listing should stop.

50

Mayday! Mayday! Mayday!

I turned on the ham radio and tuned up and down the twenty meter band searching for a strong signal. At 14309 Khz a lively conversation was in progress on the Sugar Cane Network. I waited for a momentary lull in order to break in.

At the first pause I transmitted in one word sentences:

"MAYDAY! MAYDAY! MAYDAY! THIS. IS. THE. HA-LE-A-KA-LA.
"MAYDAY! MAYDAY! MAYDAY! THIS. IS. THE. HA-LE-A-KA-LA.
"OVER."

The network conversation continued uninterrupted. I had to wait for another break. While waiting I put a life jacket on over top of the safety harness.

The next break in transmission came.

"MAYDAY! MAYDAY! MAYDAY! THIS. IS. THE. HA-LE-A-KA-LA.
"MAYDAY! MAYDAY! MAYDAY! THIS. IS. THE. HA-LE-A-KA-LA.
"OVER."

Again there was no response to my call as conversation continued on the net. At every opportunity I repeated my emergency broadcast. I became increasingly concerned that no one could hear me. Although it probably was only fifteen or

51

twenty minutes from my first Mayday call, it seemed to be forever.

As I waited for each pause in the conversation, I kept busy getting out survival gear.

Whenever I thought I might be heard, I repeated in a slow and deliberate voice:

"MAYDAY! MAYDAY! MAYDAY! THIS. IS. THE. HA-LE-A-KA-LA.
"MAYDAY! MAYDAY! MAYDAY! THIS. IS. THE. HA-LE-A-KA-LA.
"OVER."

Finally, someone heard me! A clear, although faint voice said:

"Will all traffic on this frequency cease.
"I hear a Mayday.
"Go ahead Mayday."

I looked at the coordinates displayed on the SATNAV on the table beside me and still using one word sentences in a very deliberate voice, I again repeated my call for help:

"MAYDAY! MAYDAY! MAYDAY! THIS. IS. THE. HA-LE-A-KA-LA.
"MY. POSITION. IS. ZERO. DEGREES. FORTY. NINE. MINUTES. POINT. FIVE. ZERO. NORTH. ONE. HUNDRED. SIXTY. FOUR. DEGREES. THIRTY. FIVE. MINUTES. POINT. ZERO. FOUR. WEST.

"REPEAT.
"MY. POSITION. IS. ZERO. DEGREES. FORTY. NINE. MINUTES. POINT. FIVE. ZERO. NORTH. ONE. HUNDRED. SIXTY.

FOUR. DEGREES. THIRTY. FIVE. MINUTES. POINT. ZERO. FOUR. WEST.

    "DO. YOU. READ. ME?

    "OVER."

The voice on the radio[31] responded faintly but clearly that he read my signal. Again I repeated my distress call and asked if he had also read my position.

He answered that he had received my position and read it back to me, adding: "What is the nature of your problem?"

I briefly explained my distress. When I had finished he came back on and said: "We are in contact with the Coast Guard. They will be coming up on this frequency. Stay on this frequency and you will hear directly from the Coast Guard."

Within a few moments the Coast Guard came through with a very strong transmission, which was as clear as a bell, and sounding like they were next door. I don't know how large an antenna or how much power they were using to transmit, but the signal was so strong and clear I am convinced it could be heard all the way around the world. I had no difficulty, whatsoever, hearing every word they said.

With the Coast Guard now on the frequency, I repeated my Mayday call updated with the latest reading from the SATNAV:

"MAYDAY! MAYDAY! MAYDAY! THIS. IS. THE. HA-LE-A-KA-LA.

---

[31]The mayday was first heard by Loren A. Peterson, K6EDV, in Santa Rosa, California, who established contact when he heard the distress call.

"MY. POSITION. IS. ZERO. DEGREES. FIFTY. MINUTES. POINT. ZERO. FOUR. NORTH. ONE. HUNDRED. SIXTY. FOUR. DEGREES. THIRTY. FIVE. MINUTES. POINT. ZERO. FOUR. WEST"

"REPEAT
"MY. POSITION. IS. ZERO. DEGREES. FIFTY. MINUTES. POINT. ZERO. FOUR. NORTH. ONE. HUNDRED. SIXTY. FOUR. DEGREES. THIRTY. FIVE. MINUTES. POINT. ZERO. FOUR. WEST
"DO. YOU. READ. MY. POSITION?
"OVER."

My transmission was from a 250 Watt ham transmitter, using the standing rigging of the ship as a random-wire antenna. This configuration allowed me to use the large amount of wire in the rigging to reach distant stations with relatively low power. I had been able to reach Loren Peterson[31] in California and now the Coast Guard whom I assumed to be in Honolulu. But my signal was relatively weak, and the constant motion of my antenna, as the boat moved in the water, probably made it fade in and out for them.

Apparently, my transmission was not always received clearly enough for the Coast Guard to understand everything I transmitted, because within a few minutes we had a third party radio relay station to pass on my messages. Periodically the Coast Guard would simply say: "Relay." Immediately, my words were repeated by the other station.[32]

---

[32] I later learned that WH60, apparently another American ship at sea, participated in the Mayday activity and may have been the relay station. By that time, I am sure, there were a great many other ham operators all over the world listening to the Mayday transmissions and a number of them should have been able to relay my messages.

54

As I had done from the very beginning of my Mayday call, I continued to enunciate every word clearly, separately, and distinctly to aid the reception of my message. I also tried to limit my transmissions to only the essential facts. For example, when asked for the local weather conditions, I checked them before answering. I went out on deck and observed the exact conditions at that time, using the helm compass to note the precise wind direction. I then returned to the radio and answered with an accurate synopsis, including wind speed and direction by magnetic compass and the sea conditions. I took pains to keep all my transmissions in a calm and clear voice. I did not dream at the time that this deliberate act for clear communication could, itself, have been an error.

The Coast Guard officer asked me the standard questions, starting with the number of persons aboard, the color of the hull, and what survival gear I carried. I responded to each with brief answers. "One person aboard." "Yellow hull with brown trim." When he started asking me about the safety gear I asked him to read the list and then replied "All of the above," because *Haleakala* had all of the standard safety gear including the EPIRB, emergency flares, orange smoke, emergency water, etc. He asked if I had a life raft, and I told him I had a hard dinghy (under which I had stored the two five gallon cans of emergency drinking water).

He then wanted to know how long I estimated it would be until the boat sank. I replied *Haleakala* was a catamaran and she could not sink, although she could break up. And if she did indeed break up, I would stay with the largest piece. In retrospect, I don't believe that he really understood that multihulls cannot sink and, therefore, are their own survival platform.

He advised me to put on a life jacket. I told him that I was wearing it. When he had finished the immediate questions, he asked me to stand by on this frequency and said he would contact me again in 30 minutes.

I wondered what the Coast Guard could or would do to answer a distress call from the middle of the vast Pacific Ocean.

Response

Search and rescue (SAR) commitments, authority, responsibility, operation, and conduct are addressed by a number of SAR treaties and other international instruments. To meet these international obligations as well as the domestic SAR needs, several United States agencies have cooperated to develop a National Search and Rescue Plan (NSP). In this plan, the geographic areas of U.S. SAR responsibility have been divided into regions and a Rescue Coordination Center (RCC) has been established for each region.

Response to Mayday in the Central Pacific area is assigned to the RCC in Honolulu, Hawaii, which is also designated as a Joint Rescue Coordination Center (JRCC) because it is jointly operated by Coast Guard, Air Force, and Navy personnel.[33]

---

[33]Their motto is: "WORKING TOGETHER SO OTHERS MAY LIVE."

Detailed information needed by United States federal forces, military or civilian, to implement the National Search and Rescue Plan has been consolidated into the National Search and Rescue Manual. The major SAR stages are defined in this manual as follows:

A. **Awareness.** Knowledge by any person or agency that an emergency situation may exist.

B. **Initial Action.** Preliminary action taken to alert SAR facilities and obtain amplifying information. This stage may include evaluation and classification of the information, alerting of SAR facilities, preliminary communication checks, extended communication checks, and, in urgent cases, immediate action from other stages.

C. **Planning.** The development of operational plans, including plans for search, rescue, and final delivery.

D. **Operations.** Sending Search and Rescue Units to the scene, conducting searches, rescuing survivors, assisting distressed craft, providing necessary emergency care for survivors, and delivering casualties to medical facilities.

E. **Mission Conclusion.** Return of Search and Rescue Units to a location where they are finally debriefed, refueled, replenished, re-manned, and prepared for other missions, and completion of documentation of the SAR mission by all SAR facilities.

The events in response to a Mayday are chronicled in the log of the coordinating rescue center and the logs of the various participating ships, planes, and radio operators. These logs have been used to piece together the interrelationships between the various *Haleakala* Search and Rescue activities at various locations in the Pacific Basin and continental United States. Some of those log entries are reproduced through the remaining pages of this book in order to show the detail of key events as they took place. They are also included to help convey the thinking and degree of understanding that evolved as the SAR case progressed. [Some who have read the manuscript have found these details to be interesting and deserving of further study, while others have skipped over them in the text without losing the flavor of the rescue mission.]

22 APR 0240Z (1540X): *Haleakala*, 00°49.50'N 164°35.04'W, 3:40 p.m. Mayday![34]

It was twenty minutes to four, mid afternoon on the twenty first of April, when I broadcast Mayday from *Haleakala* lying just north of the equator and 1300 nautical miles south southwest of Honolulu.

---

[34]This heading is illustrative of the headings of the events that follow. This format for the heading is used when the event can be reasonably corroborated by the log entries. Because many of the events took place in different time zones and in widely scattered geographic locations, it is easy to confuse the order of their occurrence. Therefore, a uniform system of time and place headings are used. In addition to the location and time of the event, both the local zone time and Universal Coordinated Time (Z) are indicated.

For example: In the referenced heading, the Universal Coordinated Time is indicated as two-forty a.m. on the twenty-second of April (22 APR 0240Z) which is the same time as 3:40 p.m. the previous calendar day in the time zone in which the event took place, "X" in this case, and hence 1540X is the site time given. The location of *Haleakala* is given in terms of its geographical ocean coordinates 0 degrees and almost 50 minutes north of the equator and 164 degrees and 35 minutes west of Greenwich England (00°49.50'N 164°35.04'W).

I had chosen 14309 Khz for my emergency message because I was receiving a clear signal on the Sugar Cane Network on that frequency. Although parts of my initial call may have been heard by several ham operators participating or listening to the activity on the network, they must not have recognized my message as a Mayday. Fifteen minutes later, 7:55 p.m. in California, Loren Peterson, apparently the network operator, became aware of the meaning of my call and stopped all other traffic on the frequency to listen to my Mayday.

While I was speaking to Loren in California, Tom Morgan, an off-duty radio operator stationed on the U.S. Coast Guard Cutter *Sassafras*, who was then at his home in Hawaii, also heard the message on his ham radio and immediately called the Coast Guard (COGARD) Communications Center (COMMSTA) in Honolulu. They then tuned to the Sugar Cane Network frequency and within minutes I was in direct contact with the Coast Guard. I had triggered the first SAR stage—"Awareness."

Awareness spreads rapidly in the amateur radio community; the radio signal propagates at the speed of light. When something interesting happens on the air, such as an emergency call, a great many ham operators tune in on that frequency to listen.[35] Since I had also been repeating my location, any

---

[35]There is no way to ever know the exact chain of events that led up to many ham operators listening to the conversation between the Coast Guard and the *Haleakala*, however a typical senecio might be as follows:

At the time I broke into the Sugar Cane Network to transmit my emergency, the hams listening on that frequency at the time would become aware of the event. While some would move to adjacent frequencies to discuss it, others would pass the word on to other networks that happen to be on the air at the same time but on other frequencies.

(continued...)

operator with a directional antenna could point it in the right direction to get the best possible reception. When those listening wanted to discuss the Mayday with each other, they would take care to keep off of the emergency frequency. Most often the non-interfering, immediately adjacent frequencies would be used for this communication.

22 APR 0310Z (1710W): JRCC, 5:10 p.m. SAR Alert.

As the Coast Guard Communications Station established communications with me they also began carrying out the initial actions outlined in the National SAR Manual. They contacted the Joint Rescue Coordination Center (JRCC) while speaking with me, and thereby began an official alert of the SAR forces, although no search and rescue mission was as yet established. Because of the large number of false alarms that are received, a SAR alert does not necessarily lead to a subsequent SAR mission. Additional amplifying information is needed to evaluate and classify a Mayday, to establish dire need, and to minimize response to hoaxes.

COGARD COMMSTA immediately telephoned the JRCC with the disaster details I had given them. However, it is well known that information relayed by word of mouth can be unreliable. To minimize possible confusion, the conversation between the two centers was followed by a confirming wire a half

---

[35](...continued)

Other ham operators would get the information from passively listening to the other networks, a pastime that many enjoy while waiting for a scheduled contact with another ham. Some would telephone others, particularity if they had a particular interest in maritime activities. And so on, and so on, ...

Document 1.
22 APR 0340Z (1740W) 5:40 p.m. Telex.

FROM COGARD COMMSTA HONOLULU HI
TO JRCC HONOLULU HI

SUBJECT: MARINE CRAFT INCIDENT DATA

1. HALEAKALA (REGISTRATION NUMBER 597789)
2. 0-50.4N, 164-35.04W
3. HOLE IN HULL, TAKING ON WATER
4. 22 APR 0304Z
5. 56 FOOT CATAMARAN
6. ONE PERSON ON BOARD
7. 14309.0 KHZ
8. UHF/VHF EPIRB
9. MODERATE TO ROUGH SEAS WITH MODERATE WINDS 060 DEGREES MAGNETIC
10. YES.
11. NOT AT THIS TIME
12. N/A
13. SATNAV
14. LIFE JACKETS AND DAY/NIGHT FLARES
15. TELEPHONE CALL RECEIVED FROM RADIOMAN FIRST CLASS MORGAN ADVISING OF SITUATION OF SUBJECT VESSEL AT 0307Z. MONITORED FREQUENCY AND NOTIFIED JRCC.

---

hour later.[36]

---

[36]The Telex summarizes the answers to the questions asked of all vessels in distress. The implied questions should be apparent with the exception of the following:
    4. Time of first contact (not time of Telex.)
   10. Is immediate assistance required?
   11. Is the vessel sinking?
   12. Has the vessel been boarded by the Coast Guard?

Even after this detailed marine craft incident [emergency] data had been relayed between the COGARD COMMSTA and the JRCC by phone and confirmed by telex, the situation was not yet considered a verified Mayday.[37]

To Verify a Mayday

To verify a Mayday, additional convincing evidence is needed to support a radio call for help.

Aboard *Haleakala*, the water had risen to the level of the floor boards in the port amidship stateroom while I was talking with the Coast Guard. Earlier the forward cant of the boat had kept the water from reaching the bilge drain in the aft stateroom, but now the water was sufficiently deep to cover the drain. I went out on deck to activate the corresponding bilge pump valve before returning to see what I could do to control the flooding in the staterooms below.

I returned below and immediately went to work removing the heaviest things I could find on the port side and carrying them over to the starboard side. This was to help correct the

---

[37]Later, I understood better the reluctance of the Coast Guard to activate a full Search and Rescue Mission when I found out how many false alarms they receive. I was told of one Mayday call a week or two before mine, purported to be from a ship sinking in the Pacific between California and Hawaii. Later, after a search and rescue effort had started, radio triangulation was able to show this Mayday call to be a hoax transmitted from Colorado! I simply cannot understand how anyone can get pleasure from broadcasting a false Mayday. Unfortunately, it apparently occurs quite frequently.

port list. As I worked I was worrying about the shock my Mayday would be to my poor wife. I suddenly realized I had not given the Coast Guard the telephone number where she could be reached in Honolulu. They could call Elli, and she would certainly be able to help them with any information they might need.

Elli knew absolutely everything that there was to know about *Haleakala* - even to the color of the bottom paint which she herself had applied. Her detailed information might be invaluable in a rescue attempt. I immediately went back to the radio to raise the Coast Guard. Their radio operator was off the air at the time but one of the ham operators, probably the relay station, answered my call. I told him my wife was in Honolulu and gave him the telephone number where she could be reached.

Just as I completed my message and verified he had the correct telephone number, the Coast Guard came back on frequency. He asked for the message, and I let the ham operator repeat what I had said. When my message had been relayed the Coast Guard radio operator asked: "What does he want us to tell her?"

After a moment's pause the ham operator replied: "I assume he wants you to tell her about his situation."

I returned to my re-stowing task, picking up boxes of supplies that had been stowed in the port aft stateroom and carrying them up to the starboard pilot berth. As I struggled with the heavy boxes, the water level continued to rise. When I had finished moving what I could, it was time to talk to the Coast Guard on the 30 minute check-in schedule.

I had given Elli's telephone number to the Coast Guard primarily so they would let her know what was happening, but also so she could help them with any information that might be valuable for my rescue.[38] As soon as they had the number they acted immediately.

22 APR 0317Z (1717W) 5:17 p.m. Telephone verification.

An hour and fifteen minutes after my first Mayday contact the JRCC called Elli. She was staying with our friends Abe and Sue Ablett while awaiting my arrival in Honolulu. Experienced ocean voyagers themselves, they understood and were able to give her comfort and support during her following endless hours of worry.

Abe and Sue had made the same passage from Pago Pago to Honolulu a few years before. Although they knew as well as Elli the potential dangers of my trip, particularly single-handed, they also knew that I was an experienced seaman, that *Haleakala* could not sink, and that therefore, things were not quite as bleak as they might have been. However, they also knew that I had to be in critical danger to broadcast a Mayday, and aid or rescue at my remote location in the Central Pacific was difficult if not impossible.

The JRCC called Elli not only to inform her of my peril, but also to verify they had received a genuine Mayday call; that, in fact, I had a real emergency. According to the JRCC log: "She was very emotional" and "took the news with a wavering voice."

---

[38]This telephone number was a key element for the establishment of the mission. The JRCC wanted to establish a verified Mayday before launching a SAR mission, particularly one to such a remote part of the Central Pacific.

But, most importantly, she verified that I was aboard the *Haleakala*, en route to Honolulu from Pago Pago, that the coordinates I had radioed were consistent with my expected position, and that I would not radio a Mayday without immediate threat of loss of life.

Elli answered all of their questions and gave them complete details of the ship and captain including his medical history and current health synopsis. She verified the details of survival gear aboard and assured them of my sailing competence. She provided all of this information while in shock from hearing her husband was in immediate danger of being lost at sea.

Elli made it quite clear to them that she wanted to be kept fully informed of everything, hopeful or tragic. They verified she had friends there with her and agreed to keep her completely updated on all of the developments.

The abbreviations and code words that are used in the log entry for *Haleakala*:

S/V -- "sailing vessel"

FM -- "from"

COMMSTA -- the Coast Guard communications station.

POB -- "person on board".

EPIRB -- "electronic position indicating radio beacon".

ELT -- "electronic location transmitter" here means the same thing as EPIRB.

PFD -- "personal flotation device" here referring to life jackets.

RM1 -- "radioman first class".

{H} <tel> is a deleted home telephone number.

NMO -- the radio call sign of COMMSTA

Also note that "PHONE 597-7789 (MAUI)" was in error and should have been "USCG DOCUMENTATION NUMBER 597 789," which is *Haleakala*'s documentation number issued by the Coast Guard in Honolulu.

Document 2.
22 APR 0319Z (1719W) 5:19 p.m. Opening entry of official log.

SAR Case # 043784 S/V HALEAKALA

1719W   FM COMMSTA: 56 FT CATAMARAN
         HALEAKALA TAKING ON WATER IN
         POSN 00-50-04N 164-35-04W (FM
         SATNAV) ONE POB - CHARLES COLEMAN
         ENR PAGO PAGO TO HONOLULU - PHONE
         597-7789 (MAUI). HAS EPIRB/ELT, PFD'S
         MIRROR, STROBE. BEING HANDLED BY
         RM1 TOM MORGAN (SASSAFRAS) {H} <tel>
         NMO HAS COMMS AND WILL TAKE OVER

Having established the authenticity of the mayday call, and even while still on the telephone with Elli, the JRCC now upgraded the SAR Alert to an official Search and Rescue Mission.

A REAL Emergency

I kept an eye on the clock and called the Coast Guard on schedule. They came up on frequency and reestablished contact at the appointed time.

22 APR 0330Z (1630X): *Haleakala*, 00°49'N 164°35'W, 4:30 p.m. Scheduled radio contact.

The Coast Guard operator informed me they had called Elli, were now considering this a real emergency, and were launching a Search and Rescue Mission.

A **REAL** EMERGENCY! It had never occurred to me the Coast Guard might not treat my Mayday as a real emergency. But the fact I was so calm and coherent had caused some doubt about my call until they had verified the essential facts with Elli. Apparently, some panic on my part would have made the gravity of the situation more believable, particularly since I said I was aboard a ship taking on water in the middle of the ocean. However, he had added they were "launching a Search and Rescue Mission." While I did not know exactly what that meant, I assumed, or more properly urgently hoped that it meant they were going to come and rescue me.

I related how bad things were getting aboard. As I was talking to them I gathered up rocket flares and orange smoke bombs and put them in a plastic bucket. I also put a flare gun and a handful of flare cartridges into my pockets. We scheduled our next contact again in thirty minutes.[39]

Then I looked around for Sadie. When I did not see her I made a fast search and found her in the starboard head, frightened by all the unusual happenings. I picked her up and set her out on the deck. I did not want to worry about her, but I also wanted her out of the way.

---

[39]The corresponding activity in Honolulu associated with this call is documented starting on page 80.

As I went back to my disaster preparations, I realized what a debt of gratitude I owed to the ham operators of the amateur radio service. They made it possible to communicate my dire situation to a source of help even though this help was very remote.[40]

---

[40]Most pleasure boaters rely on VHF marine radio for emergency communication, probably not realizing normal VHF reception is limited to line-of-sight reception. Even though, on occasion, I have been able to communicate with a vessel up to 50 miles away on VHF using the masthead antenna. This VHF mode of communication is useless in a Mayday situation so far from shore.

Another communication alternative is Citizens Band (CB) radio. Although not line-of-sight, CB radios are limited to five Watts radiated power, which severely restricts their range even though the Coast Guard and harbor masters in the United States monitor the CB channel number 9, the emergency channel.

Even the quite effective surface to air EPIRB is usually ineffective for long distance emergency communication because its UHF broadcast, like VHF, is also limited to line-of-sight reception. The EPIRB had been activated to communicate Mayday, line-of-sight, to any airplanes which might be flying overhead or to potentially nearby ships, although no one had yet responded to its signal.

There is one great advantage of the EPIRB over other emergency communication devices. In addition to reception by aircraft and ships, the signal can be received by an orbiting satellite and relayed to a ground station. This Search and Rescue Satellite-Aided Tracking (SARSAT) system is an internationally sponsored system of low altitude, near-polar orbiting satellites and ground receiving stations designed to provide the approximate position of EPIRB/ELT distress beacon signals. However, to do so, the relaying satellite must be simultaneously in sight of the transmitting EPIRB and the receiving station.

Unfortunately, from a position very far at sea, as I was, such a low altitude satellite relay was physically impossible. The nearest SARSAT ground station EPIRB relay receiver was at the Coast Guard Center in Honolulu more than 1300 nautical miles away. Only the infrequent passing airplane or ship would be able to receive my EPIRB signal. Although the EPIRB proved to be valuable, it was the ham radio that had made it possible to alert potential rescue forces and make them aware of my distress.

I knew things were grave, indeed, but I clung to the certain knowledge that *Haleakala* could not sink. The water had continued to rise on the port side, but the hull was not yet fully flooded. Although the boat was listing heavily, I still expected the list would stabilize when the water level reached just below the ports. At that point the wing bottom flotation would be supporting the weight of the boat and the bilge pump would be able to balance the inflow of water. However, just in case, I set the bucket of flares outside, wedged between the cabin back and the helm pedestal. I took two of the twenty or so life jackets aboard and put them out on the deck beside the flares. I also planned to go outside if there were a chance of overturning, but I still had time to check the extent of the flooding.

The port hull was now so deep in the water that the water level outside was nearly up to the ports as expected. But, totally unexpected was the fact that they were leaking! Water spurted in each time a wave lapped against the glass. Even dogged down and with the pane still intact the ports were not watertight!

I had used molded plastic ports on *Haleakala* because they were lightweight, substantial, opening ports of the traditional design.[41] But the sealed portlight did not seem to stop the water from coming through on the crest of each wave.

---

[41]The "windows" on a vessel are referred to as "ports" or, if fitted with a clear section, equally properly referred to as "portlights." Portlights can be either fixed in place or opening. The clasp which holds an opening port shut (watertight) is called a "dog." These had five dogs; three along the opening edge and one at each side. An unbreakable plastic pane, assumed to be bulletproof Lexan had been used instead of the more traditional glass. A rubber o-ring gasket was fitted around the opening window to form a seal onto which the opening port could be closed and dogged tight.

The leak was not at the seal between the hinged window frame and its base but around the Lexan pane set in the frame. When the water splashed up on the outside of the hull, some of it came pouring around the glass. Apparently the panes had been mounted into the window frame without a gasket. The frame seemed to be molded around the Lexan without permanently bonding to it, and it was impossible to see (without destroying the frame) whether or not there was an inner water seal. The plastic frame may have shrunk or warped by weathering after they had been installed which could have created gaps that were not there when they were manufactured. In any case, it is unquestionably true that the failure of the ports led to the subsequent disaster.

Now, when watertight integrity was essential, things looked very bad. All of the ports that were awash were leaking. While the flotation in the wing had slowed the degree of list, the flooding through the ports increased the problem dramatically. Where I had hoped the leak around the patch could be compensated by the bilge pump, the additional heavy flow of water around the port glass destroyed the secondary stability point. But there still remained a very slim possibility that, although the expected stable trim was not possible now, sufficient sea water might flow across, from hull to hull, through the main salon, to partially flood the starboard hull—at least enough to prevent a capsize.[42]

---

[42]The paragraph that you have just read is an accurate account of my thinking at this time. Was my reasoning correct? Since the leaking through the original hole was still occurring, even with the patch in place, would the

(continued...)

I realized that there was nothing I could do, and time was short. I picked up a large strobe-light from the helm supply shelf, fastened it to my harness and headed for the companionway. I needed to be out on deck if *Haleakala* should indeed roll over. I knew Sadie had not come back inside because I had kept half an eye on her. I stepped out through the companionway clipping on as I always did and looked for Sadie. She was on the starboard catwalk staring at the ocean and mewing her bewilderment at the rolling sea.

I went over to the high side of the boat with Sadie and moved my safety line from the mizzen shroud to the top lifeline. Clipping on was second nature, a part of subconscious safety conditioning.

As I was trying to anticipate what would happen the boat suddenly listed hard to port, gunnel awash, and then slowly came back. Then again she rolled over further to port, and, again, very slowly came up. Then suddenly I realized that this was it. She rolled further and further, picking up speed, then in a rush, over all the way, throwing Sadie into the water and pulling me deep beneath the surface!

---

[42](...continued)
additional flow around the portlights make a noticeable difference? Probably not, but leaking portlights were now my focus of attention, not the forward hole.

The expected mental state of a victim reacting to the trauma of a disaster is reviewed in the epilogue starting on page 255.

Dragged Underwater

When *Haleakala* turned over I was dragged underwater by my safety line still clipped to the upper lifeline! And, because I was wearing a large, man-sized life jacket which was very effective in attempting to raise me to the surface, I received a nearly fatal safety lesson! With the strong upward pull of the life jacket and the long length of the safety line, I was unable to reach the shackle to unfasten myself from the lifeline, and I was being held underwater! My safety rule, to wear a harness and to remain clipped on at all times while on deck, was a terrible error and under the circumstances, the error was now threatening to rapidly become a fatal mistake.

At the moment of confusion when we overturned I gasped, I may have yelled, and I don't know whether I was inhaling or exhaling as I went down. But I could not have lasted longer than one last gulp of air would allow had I not been wearing the standard "Charley's Safety Gear" consisting of light, whistle, and KNIFE—the trusty knife I always wore on a lanyard around my neck. I quickly opened the knife, cut the line, and popped up to the surface gasping for air.

I had always considered the knife to be an important piece of my safety equipment, and I found constant use for it, but its importance became a life-or-death matter—it was the critical item that had just saved me from drowning. In addition, I had also just learned another new safety lesson:

THERE SHOULD BE A SNAP SHACKLE AT BOTH ENDS OF SAFETY HARNESS LINES.

In addition to the standard shackle at the far end, a second shackle is needed to attach the safety line to the harness. This way the safety line can be detached from the harness if it fouls and endangers the wearer. This additional shackle modification reestablished the validity of wearing a harness and keeping a safety line attached to the boat while on deck. I'll never sail again without shackles on both ends of my safety lines.

When I reached the surface, Sadie was swimming away from the boat, clearly trying to get away from the noise and havoc behind her. I called to her and swam toward her. She stopped swimming, and when I reached her I put her up behind me on the back of my life jacket and turned to swim back to the overturned boat.

Already, as I swam back, I saw many of my possessions floating in the water around me, now just flotsam. Books from the bookcase near the chart table were barely floating and sank out of sight as I watched. But I was so happy that I had been able to save myself from drowning and had gotten Sadie safely on the back of my life jacket, that I did not dwell on the mere loss of all my worldly possessions.

When I reached the boat, I swam around to the stern and climbed up on the wing bottom which now rose a couple of feet above the water. I put Sadie up on the starboard keel (which was now on the left side)[43] and stopped to catch my breath and to make some kind of plans for survival.

Sunset was rapidly approaching, and I pondered about the terrible spot we were in. A few short hours ago I had felt safe and certainly comfortable aboard *Haleakala*. Now I realized that Sadie and I were in for a night exposed to the elements on the capsized *Haleakala*, and anything more that I needed to do had to be done quickly. Darkness falls suddenly after sundown in the tropics.

I was wearing just what I happened to have on that day. Clothing is worn in the tropics mainly for social reasons, as little weather protection is required. When at sea in tropical waters, many sailors dispense with clothes altogether. But at night, although only fifty miles from the equator where the air is relatively mild, my soaked clothes gave me a chill, and poor Sadie was shivering in my arms. At that moment I would have welcomed a little more weather protection.

I still had my personal safety gear: my life jacket over my harness, knife, whistle, waterproof flashlight, and a large strobe light. The flare gun and extra flares were still in my pockets. The bucket of flares I had set out on deck was long gone in the deep. However, the two extra life jackets I had put on deck

---

[43]The port/starboard nomenclature remains regardless of the orientation of the vessel, including the upside down position.

Note that the two hulls of a catamaran already add confusion to the directional nomenclature of the parts of a ship. For example, the structural member that ties the deck to the hull is called a shear-clamp. A monohull has a port shear-clamp and a starboard shear-clamp. However, there are four different shear-clamps on a catamaran referred to as: the starboard outboard shear-clamp, the starboard inboard shear-clamp, the port inboard shear-clamp, and the port outboard shear-clamp.

were floating nearby, and I retrieved them as well as a piece of line trailing from underneath. I looked at the flotsam in the water but could not see anything else of possible value. Night was rapidly descending on us.

SAR Forces

While on the capsized boat my fate was in the hands of the JRCC. Potential rescue forces had been alerted and initial actions had already been taken when the COMMSTA first received the Mayday call. With the Alert now upgraded to a SAR Mission, the center completed the Initial Actions Phase and began the SAR Planning Phase.[44] At this point they started marshalling SAR forces, those individual resources needed for the mission. Of immediate importance was the identification of airplanes and ships in the Mayday call area that could look for a vessel in distress.

Mid-ocean search and rescue missions require resources with capabilities much beyond those needed for the more frequent coastal rescues. Near land, helicopters and small planes can be used effectively to locate and assist disabled or foundering vessels. Coast Guard boats and small pleasure craft can get to such Mayday sites quickly. But helicopters and small aircraft do not have sufficient range to respond to a deep sea Mayday, and

---

[44]The major SAR stages are outlined on page 57.

help from surface vessels can only come from the ships that happen to be in the vicinity of the shipwreck.

Obviously, it is important to locate any survivors and wreckage as soon as possible when a Mayday is received in order to treat wounds and minimize exposure. But, in addition to the need to render fast medical assistance, the problem of locating any survivors at sea becomes increasingly difficult as time passes. A patch of flotsam that would help would-be rescuers locate survivors is dispersed by wave and wind action, becoming less visible from the air as time passes. Most importantly, the direction and speed of movement of anything (or anyone) floating in the water cannot be predicted with great accuracy.[45]

All mid-ocean SAR missions start with some degree of uncertainty in the location of potential survivors and the estimated uncertainty determines the size of the search area. As time goes on without sighting the target, the degree of uncertainty grows and the corresponding area to cover grows geometrically. To a first approximation, when the time doubles, the area that needs to be searched to achieve a given level of confidence quadruples.

With satellite-tracking of the EPIRB ruled out because of the remote location of the Mayday site, the initial search plan for the *Haleakala* called for rapid location of the stricken vessel from the air by electronic and visual means. Location of an EPIRB from the air is most easily done by a high altitude

---

[45]Experiments in which multiple test bottles have been dropped into the sea at the same place and time have shown the bottles to have washed ashore at different times and in completely different parts of the world.

overflight by a plane equipped with a radio direction finder (RDF). The area covered by a high altitude flight is much greater than the area covered by a low altitude flight.[46] A visual search at night requires a quite low overflight by a slower plane equipped with flares and searchlights.

High altitude, extra-long-range, RDF equipped, jet aircraft suitable as SAR units can be assigned to the mission by the Navy, Air Force, and/or commercial airlines. Accordingly, the JRCC requested SAR force availability from the Navy Third Fleet at Pearl Harbor, the Air Force at Hickam Air Force Base, and the Federal Aviation Administration (FAA) Air Route Traffic Control Center (ARTCC) in Honolulu.

22 APR 0330Z (1730W): 5:30 p.m. Navy response.

The first response to the request for available SAR forces came from the U.S. Navy Third Fleet. Within minutes of the initial alert, the Navy advised the JRCC that they had no planes and no vessels[47] in the Mayday area at that time.

22 APR 0349Z (1749W): 5:49 p.m. Air Force response.

The U.S. Air Force Command Post at Hickam Field responded to the SAR mission with a recommendation for the

---

[46]A high altitude electronic search flight covers more than twenty five times as much area as a low level visual search flight.

[47]Although the US Navy is unmatched in sea-power, the number of navy vessels at sea at any one time, is much less than the number of commercial vessels at sea at the same time.

use of a Military Airlift Command (MAC) flight for the SAR mission. The JRCC then contacted the Pacific Airlift Command Center (PALCC) at Hickam Air Force Base to request availability of MAC resources.

22 APR 0355Z (1755W): 5:55 p.m. FAA response.

The FAA reported they had record of only one flight within range of the reported position of *Haleakala*. A commercial airliner, Air Pacific Flight 551, was currently en route from Honolulu to Nandi, Fiji, on a flight plan that could take it within six hundred nautical miles of the stricken vessel. Consequently the JRCC requested Flight 551 be diverted to overfly 00°50'N 164°35'W and be asked to listen for an EPIRB broadcasting on 121.5 Mhz. Twenty-five minutes later, Aeronautical Radio, Inc., which maintains contact with airliners aloft, relayed the message to the plane to divert and overfly the Mayday site.

It was now after dark in Honolulu with only the commercial plane overflight in preparation while PALCC was trying to locate a MAC flight for the search. In addition, whether or not *Haleakala* was located by electronic search, several patrol planes were needed for continuous coverage, and a surface vessel was needed for the rescue attempt.

Continuous air coverage at such a deep ocean Mayday site requires at least three patrol aircraft. While one was on patrol providing coverage, another would be en route to or from the site, and the third would be on the ground being refueled and serviced. Thus three or more patrol planes had to be located and arrangements made for refueling and servicing them, if continuous coverage was to be provided. Not only does such mid-ocean effort require three planes, they also must be very-long-range[48] aircraft. The C-130 Hercules[49] has proven valuable as such a very-long-range SAR aircraft. However, *Haleakala* was well beyond the normal radius-of-action of very-long-range aircraft and just barely within the operational limit of a C-130 dispatched from their closest base of operation.

C-130's are flown by the Coast Guard from the Air Station at Barbers Point, the USAF 6594th TEST Group at Hickam, and other SAR groups throughout the country including the 41st Rescue and Weather Reconnaissance Wing at McClellan Air Force Base, California, and the 23rd Air Force at Scott Air Force Base, Illinois. The JRCC immediately briefed the Air Station at Barbers Point and contacted the 6594th for available C-130's.

Although aircraft are very effective in searching for a stricken vessel and particularly in locating an EPIRB, a surface vessel is still needed on the scene for the actual rescue of survivors. All vessels are potential elements of search and rescue forces. Even incidental pleasure boat skippers are generally

---

[48]A very-long-range aircraft has a normal radius-of-action of 1000 nautical miles or more from the land based SAR facilities. This radius-of-action is determined by the plane's ability to fly to the scene, remain on the scene as long as required, and to return to base with sufficient fuel reserve.

[49]The C-130 cruises at just under 300 knots. It carries enough fuel to fly a maximum of 15 hours with a maximum one-way range of 4400 nautical miles, a normal radius-of-action of 1200 miles, and an operational limit of 1400 nautical miles.

aware of the rescue responsibilities they assume as master of a vessel.[50]

To capitalize on the SAR capability of any vessel in the area, a distress notice to mariners was prepared, and the distress broadcast began in response to the wire illustrated as Document 3.

Even while the distress broadcast wire was being sent from the JRCC, COMMSTA was expecting my next scheduled broadcast on 14309 Khz. I had last spoken to them at 5:30 p.m., Honolulu time, and I had agreed to call them for a second check-in thirty minutes later. It was now only forty minutes since the *Haleakala* SAR Case had been opened.

When no call was received as scheduled, COMMSTA called me, but, of course, received no answer. Repeated attempts were made to contact me. By ten minutes after six COMMSTA had concluded that I either could not broadcast or I was transmitting but had insufficient power for them to hear my signal. At this point, seven additional radio operators took turns trying to raise me. Then the fact that I had missed the scheduled radio contact was reported by COMMSTA to the JRCC.[51]

---

[50]The responsibilities are imposed by a number of international treaties and conventions, here specifically the Convention on Safety of Life at Sea (SOLAS 1960), supported by the United States.

SOLAS 1960 obligates the master of any vessel at sea who becomes aware of a Mayday distress to attempt to render assistance. He must proceed to the site and assist the distressed vessel unless and until he is aware other aid is at hand. Once on site, he must render assistance and continue aid until the vessel in distress releases him from further obligation.

[51]The JRCC logged this as "the last transmission from vessel in distress," 5:30 p.m. Hawaiian time.

Document 3.
22 APR 0357Z (1757W): 5:57 p.m. Telex.

FROM JRCC HONOLULU HI
TO COGARD COMMSTA HONOLULU HI

SUBJECT: DISTRESS 56 FOOT CATAMARAN TAKING ON
WATER BROADCAST

MAKE DISTRESS BROADCAST IN ACCORDANCE WITH
INTERNATIONAL TELECOMMUNICATIONS UNION
BROADCAST REGULATIONS ON 500 KHZ, 2182 KHZ UPON
RECEIPT, FIRST SILENT PERIOD, AND EVERY THIRTY
MINUTES THEREAFTER UNTIL CANCELED. UTILIZE AUTO
ALARM ON FIRST AND SECOND BROADCAST ONLY.

QUOTE:

THE SAILING VESSEL HALEAKALA HAS BEEN REPORTED
TAKING ON WATER IN POSITION 00-5--04N 164-35-04W.
HALEAKALA IS A FIFTY SIX FOOT CATAMARAN WITH ONE
PERSON ON BOARD. ALL MARINERS IN AREA ARE
REQUESTED TO DIVERT AND ASSIST IF POSSIBLE.

SIGNED U.S. COAST GUARD HONOLULU

UNQUOTE

A major break came when PALCC reported they had located a potential search plane, a C-141 en route to American Samoa. The plane required two hours to be serviced on the ground in Pago Pago but then would be able to fly to the equator to arrive at *Haleakala* by 10 o'clock at the earliest (11 p.m. in Honolulu).[52]

Weather data are important to SAR planning, and there followed a routine call to the Weather Bureau for the current weather conditions at the Mayday site and the forecast for the next forty-eight hours. The specific wind direction and speed are critical elements of a SAR plan because of the need to predict the drift of shipwreck survivors, while cloud cover and precipitation affect search procedure planning.

The Flight Weather Center reported that there were scattered thunder-showers over the site with the ceiling broken or overcast. The two-day forecast was for the wind to continue from the east northeast at eight to fifteen knots accompanied by seas four to seven feet with a period of seven seconds.

22 APR 0720Z (2120W): 9:20 p.m. Overflight report.

Aeronautical Radio called the JRCC to report they had received a message from the diverted airliner. Air Pacific 551 reported it had overflown the Mayday position, 0°50'N 164°35'W, and was unable to detect any EPIRB signal on 121.5 Mhz. This was bad news. Flight 551 constituted the first search, and the results were to be used to plan any subsequent searches. Assuming 551 had vectored to and flown over the given position and that the position I had given was accurate, lack of a signal from the EPIRB implied loss of the vessel and

---

[52]The C-141 is a high-altitude, very-long-range military cargo and passenger air transport turbojet that cruises at about 450 knots. It has an aft cargo bay door much like the C-130 and is capable of making an air drop.

no survivors. From the operational altitude of a commercial jet, a properly functioning EPIRB should be able to be detected 200 miles away. The only logical conclusion, given the validity of these facts, was that there was no survivor with an operational EPIRB within tens of thousands of square miles around the reported Mayday site.

[I am thankful this bad news did not stop the SAR mission now underway and the MAC overflight being arranged by PALCC was not canceled. Further EPIRB and visual searches were still planned at that time. However, this failure of early detection of the EPIRB by Flight 551 significantly increased the circle of doubt around my position and implied a correspondingly larger (and growing) SAR search area. In short, the problem of locating any survivor had become considerably more difficult due to the fact that Air Pacific Flight 551 had not confirmed the EPIRB position.]

Raft *Haleakala*

Overturned in mid-ocean, the Yacht *Haleakala* had now become the "Raft *Haleakala*." She was no longer capable of sailing although she still was my refuge and possible means of survival. Although I had only a few things with me, beneath my feet were all the survival equipment, food, water, and supplies that would ever be needed. My first priority was to get the emergency water bottles stowed outside under the dinghy on the aft deck. They would be a lot easier to retrieve than anything from inside the boat.

The problem with retrieving the additional supplies from inside the boat was that I would have to dive down, enter the boat underwater, get what I needed, and exit the same way without breathing. I didn't see how I could make the round trip in less that a couple of minutes, and that would be an awfully long time for me to hold my breath.

I slipped into the water to dive under the stern section of the false wing to get at the emergency water. Acid was leaking into the water from the banks of large batteries in the engine compartment and under the companionway steps, and Diesel fuel was spilling from the fuel tanks. Together they made it extremely painful and nearly impossible to open my eyes underwater. Also the short dusk had turned to pitch black. Unable to see, I climbed out of the water and clipped my remaining safety line around the prop shaft and back to my harness, having learned the new safety lesson. I would have to make do with what I had until daylight.

A snorkel and mask would have allowed me to go under the wing and get the fresh water and would have given me extra time to get other supplies, but I had left them in the port forward stateroom when working on the patch. I had assumed that I would need them again when I returned to caulk the patch. I could now see that a mask and snorkel as well as swimming fins are another valuable if not essential part of survival gear.

It was time to rest while I reconsidered my actions since I first heard the big bang. I should have launched the dinghy and would have with even one other person aboard. I could have put the emergency water and flares and even food in the dinghy and trailed it behind the boat on the painter. These emergency supplies would have been an ace in the hole if disaster were to befall us as it had. However, I knew that the boat could not sink, and since I was only responsible for myself and Sadie, my efforts that afternoon had been concentrated on also saving *Haleakala*.

Another person aboard might even have made possible the saving of *Haleakala*. He or she would surely have discovered the leak amidships before I did. Early detection could have made it possible to reduce the flow around the bulkhead by caulking and/or using the hull patching trick of sail material and a gallon or two of paint. This could have bought enough additional time to affect greater repairs to the hole and the gouge along the side.

By the time I discovered that the portlights were leaking, it was probably too late to launch the dinghy, although there may still have been a slim chance that I might have had time after exiting from the cabin. There were very few minutes before the capsize and launching a nine foot hard dinghy by myself was somewhat time consuming even from its more convenient aft cradle rather than its former spot on the forward net. It still entailed using the mizzen halyard for a launching davit. Even in panic, I don't think I could have just lifted the dinghy over the rail and into the water. But I blame my eternal optimism for not giving it a try!

With the coming of night it was time to make the raft as comfortable as possible for Sadie and me. When I built *Haleakala* I had extended the main deck aft and had made a single thickness false wing where other catamarans have an aft net. There I mounted a folding boarding ladder which could be lowered for use either as a swimming step or for climbing in and out of the shore tender. It was still lashed in place, but could be extended up in the direction of the prop and rudder. I untied the lines holding the ladder to the aft compression beam and unfolded it up against the hull lashing it to the prop shaft. With the ladder held in this position, I could use it to rest on and to climb out of the water swirling around my feet.

Occasional waves lapped over the leading edge of the wing, rushed back the length of the boat, and then ran off the stern. Every ten minutes or so the top of a large wave would curl over the bow, creating a line of surf and breaking over my legs as I stood on the wing bottom. The waves were still building and reached about six to seven feet by morning. This surf tended to knock me off my feet as I stood there, and I wanted to get up on the keel and out of the breakers.

Sadie kept watching me from where I had put her on the keel. She had stopped complaining, although I am sure she was not happy with the strange events. She was still soaking wet and shivering from her swim. With little else to do now but to think and observe, I wanted to cradle Sadie in my arms to comfort her and in turn, she could comfort me.

I took one of the extra life jackets and wedged it between the prop and the rudder to serve as a cushion and climbed up the boarding ladder beside Sadie. I thought the best place to put the large strobe light was on my back while still keeping it fastened to my harness by the lanyard. It would be visible there in all directions except dead ahead. But with all the motion back and forth it should even be visible from straight ahead most of the time. And on my back it would not be as blinding to us.

I tried to rest in this position with Sadie in my arms but rather than trying to sleep, I spent most of the time assessing everything that I could about my new environment. This knowledge might help me survive. I knew the means of survival were there if I could just figure out how best to use them.

MAC-38084

The Pacific Airlift Command Center at Hickam Air Force Base in Honolulu had assigned the SAR mission to MAC-38084, a C-141 of the 63rd Military Air Wing, Norton Air Force Base, California.

MAC-38084 was now being serviced on the ground in Pago Pago, American Samoa. This plane was to search for the *Haleakala* by EPIRB-RDF and flares and be prepared to drop a survival raft. However, a problem had arisen. The plane did not have an appropriate survival life raft aboard, one which was designed to be dropped from the air. The crew had been trying to locate such a raft in Pago Pago, but had been unable to find one. PALCC was notified and they, in turn, asked the JRCC to see if the Coast Guard could locate a suitable raft in American Samoa.

It had been a couple of years since the Coast Guard Station in Pago Pago had been closed and the responsibility and resources turned over to the Government of American Samoa. Now only a Coast Guard Liaison Office staffed by Lieutenant

Junior Grade DeJong remained, and the JRCC attempted to contact him.

It was after seven in the evening in Samoa and even though at first the liaison officer could not be found, a message was left for him that a survival raft, designed to be air dropped, was needed for MAC-38084. Such a raft might still be found aboard the former Coast Guard rescue vessel now operated by the Territorial Government or at the FAA facilities at the Pago Pago airport.

Shortly after the message was left, Lt. DeJong returned the call saying he had searched for an appropriate life raft but had been unable to locate one anywhere on the island. MAC-38084 would have to use one of the rafts it had aboard for emergency ditching at sea.

A short time later the JRCC received word that MAC-38084 had been officially approved for the SAR flight and the crew was waiting to be briefed. At a quarter to eight, Pago Pago time, the JRCC briefed PALCC for MAC-38084 and they, in turn, immediately briefed the crew, and shortly the plane prepared for take-off from Pago Pago without the needed survival life raft aboard.

As MAC-38084 was taxiing for take-off from Pago Pago, the report arrived from Air Pacific Flight 551 that it had overflown the Mayday site, no EPIRB had been heard, and no wreckage or survivor had been sighted. Nevertheless, MAC-38084 lifted off. They had nearly 1000 nautical miles to fly to the equator to search for wreckage.

22 APR 0745Z (2145W) 9:45 p.m.

After flight MAC-38084 left the ground, PALCC reported to JRCC the flight was, in fact, airborne with an estimated two and a half hours until arrival on station.

PALCC also reported that they had located a C-130 patrol plane which would be upcoming with crew from the 22nd Air Force Group, Travis Air Force Base, California.

Headway to Weather

Trying to rest atop the overturned hull while concentrating on finding a means of survival, I was struck by the fact that *Haleakala* was making headway to weather. Even upside down, with only the two hulls above the water, and without any sails to catch the wind, she was indeed making progress. As I watched the motion, I worked out how she was able to sail in this inverted position. It was similar to the "disappearing whale" problem[53] of the old whaling days.

---

[53]Whales were hunted from small whale boats which spread out from a large factory mother ship. When a whale was harpooned from the whale boat, unable to tow it with the small boat, the whalers would have to bring back the mother ship to retrieve and process the whale. Frequently, they would return with the ship to find that the whale was gone.

The problem was that the dead whale would "swim" away before the whalers could return with the ship. Dead whales do swim! The motion of the waves flowing over the body makes the tail move with a flapping motion which generates a forward momentum, even though there are no muscular contractions.

(continued...)

But, while dead whales (with tails) swim in random directions, *Haleakala* was maintaining a course directly up weather into the wind! The main difference between the dead whale "swimming" and the boat's motion was due to the vessel being pointed into the wind by the weather vane effect of the rudders. The large, high-lift rudders were mounted near the stern of the ship and extended below (now above) the hull. The ten square foot area of each was effective in keeping the bow pointed into the wind.

The wind blowing over the ocean tends to kick up waves in lines perpendicular to the wind. With the bow pointed to weather, the resulting wave lines reinforced to give the boat a strong hobby-horse like motion. As the raft pitched down it would plunge into a rising wave causing the water to roll over the leading edge of the wing. Then, as it pitched up again, the wave ran down the length of the wing, creating a line of surf while driving the boat forward, before running off the trailing edge back into the sea. The wind vane effect of the rudders held the direction of travel while the porpoising motion drove *Haleakala* forward through the water so it could make headway up wind.

In addition to the effect of this forward motion on the surface, the boat was also moving along with the equatorial

---

[53](...continued)
Once whalers learned this, they cut off the tail flukes of the dead whales which kept them from swimming away.

current[54] which flows to the west. This current was most probably stronger than the forward speed of the *Haleakala* raft so passage over the bottom would still be to the west. In order to determine our actual drift I needed to calculate our relative speed through the water.

To do this I had to determine the time it took to cover a measured distance. As we moved ahead in the dark of night, we created a clearly visible wake of phosphorescence starting near the bow. I was able to pick out a patch of "sparkling" water near the bow and keep track of the same patch of water by the bubbles and phosphorescence as it moved along the length of the hull. The length of *Haleakala* is 56 feet as measured from the bow to the end of the transom. If I could time the same patch of water from the bow until it was four feet aft of the transom we would have traveled a total of sixty feet.

Measuring the time it took for the bubbles to move past was easy. My watch, which I still wear, has a built-in stopwatch which I used to time the sixty foot travel.[55] I repeated the measurements a number of times and found some expected variation in speed. The time varied from slightly over one minute to slightly under one and a half minutes.

---

[54]The presence of the current had been verified by the SATNAV calculations at noon.

[55]Although the watch has a built-in light, I found that it was much easier to use my flashlight to read the time after I had made a measurement. The watch holds the measured time between "start" and "stop" until "reset" is pushed.

The simple speed calculations from these figures were easy to do in my head.[56]   Therefore, the average speed of Raft *Haleakala* was one half knot plus or minus one tenth of a knot.

The next problem was to determine the direction in which we were sailing. With a SATNAV aboard, I no longer routinely navigated manually by sextant. I should have kept in continuous practice with sightings and manual calculations regardless of all the electronic gadgets aboard, but I had come to trust[57] my completely waterproof and submersible SATNAV.

Using the orientation of Orion to estimate north and the Celestial Equator, I estimated that we were sailing a little north of east and swinging back and forth over about a twenty degree heading change as our "weather vane" sought the wind. For the last couple of days before the capsizing we had been on a starboard tack, hard on the weather, on a course of about 20

---

[56]A nautical mile is roughly 6000 feet (actually 6076 feet), which is 100 times the length of the boat (including the extra four feet I added). If it took a minute to travel one boat length, it would take 100 times as long or 100 minutes to travel one nautical mile. Since it takes 60 minutes to cover one nautical mile (or 100 boat lengths) at 1 knot, and only 60 lengths were actually covered in a hour, then the speed could be calculated as $60/100 = 0.6$ knots. When it took a minute and a half to cover one boat length, it would take 150 minutes to go a nautical mile or $60/150 = 0.4$ knots.

[57]I had tested the SATNAV at anchor and found it to be accurate and consistent. It was so good, in fact, that when a discrepancy appeared between the SATNAV and the charted position of an island, the SATNAV was invariably correct. For example, we had just left American Samoa which I found to be a half mile south of its chart position! The charts of Samoa turned out to be based on the Japanese datum which is known to be biased by the proximity of Mount Fuji. The satellite fix of the island was more accurate than the surveyed position.

The world's charts are being updated to correspond to the more uniform and reproducible navigation satellite datum rather than the various land based surveying data in use until now.

degrees true. Since *Haleakala* could "tack in ninety," the true wind must have been at about 80 degrees which would be consistent with the estimated heading.

I had done my best to determine the speed and direction in which Raft *Haleakala* was sailing. But I wondered how accurate my calculations were and whether I had made any mistakes.

The Constellation of Orion which I had used for the celestial equator was nearly overhead, and I decided to also use it as a star clock; to watch it move across the night sky until it reached the horizon and thereby marked the time as midnight. Although I was wearing an accurate watch, I did not want to waste the valuable batteries of the flashlight to keep checking the time when I had the original clock all about me in the form of the dazzling celestial sphere. Watching the stars in the quiet of night made me feel more in tune with my surroundings and gave me some peace and comfort. From where I was, nearly every star in the sky could be seen sooner or later, with the possible exception of Polaris. Tonight low tropical squall clouds obscured the stars near the horizon, so I could not identify any of the stars in the Southern Cross or the Dippers.

I cradled Sadie in my arms and spoke quietly to her. I told her where we were and how bad our situation had become. She purred in response as I stroked her. I also tried to get comfortable on my perch with Sadie nestled in my arms. Even with an extra life jacket padding the prop, it was a hopeless cause. Every hour or so, I had to put Sadie on the keel and get down on the ladder to stretch my cramped muscles. I would stand on the ladder awhile to let the circulation return before climbing back up to try a different position, wedged behind the prop.

I think that Sadie got more sleep than I did during these hours while I comforted her. She had shaken or licked most of the water from her fur so that it was no longer matted, and she seemed reasonably comfortable while I was shivering from the spray kicked up by the wind blowing over us. My legs, arms, and head were bare, and the life jacket was open on the sides and bulked out in front away from my chest. Still it provided some warmth. I considered getting back in the water because the ocean was actually warmer than the air, but I did not want to stay soaked with salt water. I reasoned that by staying out of the water my clothes would dry somewhat and make me more comfortable.

I continued to speak aloud to Sadie, both to comfort her and to put my thoughts in order. I told her I knew I had been able to get off a distress signal and that I had talked to the Coast Guard on the ham band. They had assured me that they were going to handle my mayday as a "real emergency," and I hoped and prayed that they meant that there would be some major effort to rescue us.

I had no idea of the procedures of a rescue. I imagined that they might use a flying boat[58] to land and pick us up. Not realizing their limited range, I also thought perhaps a helicopter would fly from the nearest island (Christmas Island). And, of course, I hoped that there was a ship traveling between Honolulu and Pago Pago at the time, although I knew that ships are few and far between even on the "heavily traveled" shipping

---

[58]But has anyone seen any flying boats lately?

lanes, with the exception of the few places where shipping lanes converge just offshore.

On the overturned *Haleakala*, thinking of the difficulty of even an attempted rescue, I was acutely aware of the vastness of the ocean to me now like the impossible vastness of space. Imagine trying to locate a particular small house somewhere in the central part of the United States or even just somewhere on land. My little 25 by 56 foot raft was that insignificant in the largest body of water on a planet that is mostly water. I knew from my own experience just how vast the Pacific Ocean is. All of the land area of the entire world is less than the area of the Pacific. Not only that, but there would be enough Pacific Ocean area left over to just about fit in North America a second time.

Suddenly, as I was daydreaming about the vast ocean and rescue, the ladder broke beneath me. The hinge joint failed due to the strain of being tied at such an unusual angle. With a sudden reflex, I caught it with my foot, grabbed it before it could get away, and jumped down to fix it. I retied the broken half of the ladder to the prop shaft making a step with it that was low enough for me to stand on and yet high enough to be out of the major part of the spray. I again leaned over the hull trying another resting position and drifted off so that I actually got a few moments of sleep while more or less standing up.

AMVER System

The general broadcast seeking assistance from any vessel at sea was being repeated every half hour over the international distress frequencies of 500 kHz and 2182 kHz (see the telex on page 81), and already the Navy had reported that they had no vessels that were near enough to the scene to be able to aid *Haleakala*. Now the Automated Mutual-Assistance Vessel Rescue System (AMVER) was used to determine the identity and location of merchant vessels closest to the reported position of *Haleakala*.

Table II. Surface Picture for 00°50'N 164°35'W

#	CALL	NAME	POSITION	TP	HRS	DIST	COURSE	SAR-DATA	FG		REG
1	A8TF	ATLANTIC RAINBOW	05.3N 177.5W	VV	54.9	823.42	020.1	HX R T VXZS	LI		PAC02
2	D5NZ	POLYNESIA	15.1S 166.4W	VV	57.8	960.04	006.4	H8 R T VXZS	KPH LI		PAC02
3	DICQ	COLUMBUS QUEENSLAND	00.4N 180.0W	VV	49.6	927.60	138.5	H8 R T VXZ	VIS GE		PAC02
4	ELCW6	STOLT VENTURE	01.0S 177.0W	VV	56.1	757.23	137.4	HX R T VXZS	LGB LI		PAC02
5	H9KJ	GAMA PALA	04.8S 176.6W	VV	57.2	801.06	165.2	HX R T VXZS	LGB PN		PAC02
6	WTEA	DISCOVERER	05.0S 170.0W	AA	34.1	476.74	043.1	H8 R T VXZS	GKA US		PAC02

AMVER is a computer based, international, maritime position-reporting system operated by the United States Coast Guard. The computer maintains the current position and characteristics of each participating vessel which may be a valuable resource for SAR missions. All U.S. merchant vessels and many other participating vessels periodically transmit their latest position, course, and speed to be entered into the AMVER computer. These figures are then used to generate and maintain confidential dead reckoning positions for every vessel in the system. All information maintained by the system about a vessel known to be within an area of interest is made available upon request to recognized SAR agencies of any nation or to any vessel needing assistance. However, the current locations of vessels may only be disclosed to others for marine safety purposes.

AMVER refers to the report of vessel positions as a "surface picture." The surface picture of the six closest vessels to *Haleakala* listed only one, the U.S. registry National Oceanic and Atmospheric Administration Ship (NOAAS) *Discoverer*, to be within 500 miles of position 00°50'N 164°35'W and the remaining five ships ranging from over 750 miles to almost 1000 miles from *Haleakala*. Figure 9 shows the positions of the vessels plotted on (and beyond) a greatly reduced copy of Chart 541 using the AMVER Surface Picture vessel number to identify and mark the location of each vessel and the shipwreck symbol for *Haleakala*. Beyond the six, the next nearest vessels were tuna purse seiners at anchor in Pago Pago Harbor a thousand miles away. (No AMVER vessels were at either Christmas Island or Palmyra Island.)

The small square[59] just below the middle of the chart outlines the disaster site with a plot of the boundaries to be used for the search and rescue effort. (This square appears greatly magnified in later figures.)

---

[59]The 14,400 square nautical miles in this square is about twice the area of the State of Massachusetts. The SAR mission is to locate within this vast area the wreckage of a vessel no larger than a house and then to rescue the lone occupant.

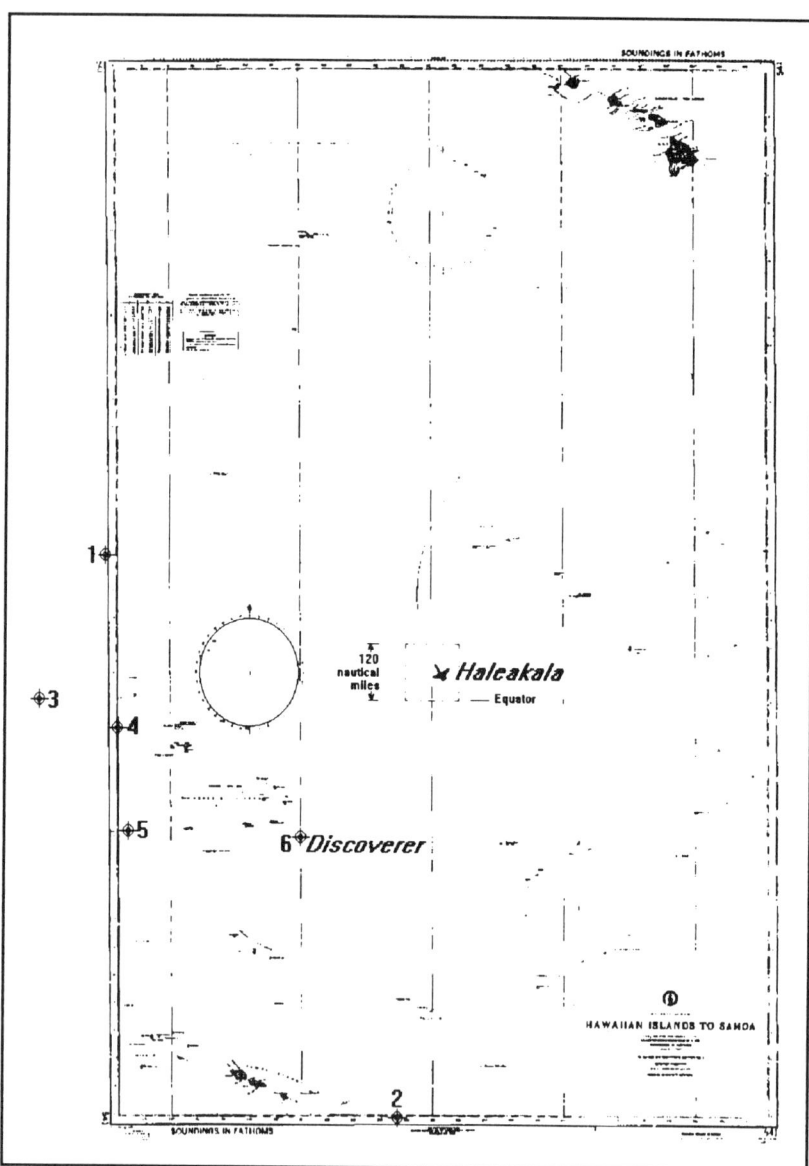

Figure 9   **Surface Picture Plotted on Chart 541.**

Based on the cruising speed entered for *Discoverer*, the AMVER system further predicted she could be at the Mayday site in less than a day and a half by sailing on a course of 043 degrees from her present position. The predicted times to

Document 4.

Additional SAR information on *Discoverer*.

```
                    WTEA/CALL

             CALL : = WTEA
             NAME : = DISCOVERER
             FLAG : = US
          RIG/SVC : = DEX
   LAST BOARDED : = 17 11 78

        LINE CODE : = NOAA
           LENGTH : = 0303
             TONS : = 003701
        SAR DATA : = H8 R T VXZS
          RADSTA : = GKA

   CONTROL TIME : = 840422.2100
        POSITION : = 05.0S 170.0W
             CSE : = 000.0
             SPD : = 14.0
     DEST / POS : = OPAREA / 05.0S 170.0W
   PREDICTED ETA : = 840421.1400
```

station for the remaining nearby vessels were from two to two and a half days.

Additional SAR information on *Discoverer*, keyed on her radio call sign "WTEA," was accessed from AMVER and the resulting report is shown as Document 4.[60]

---

[60]The additional SAR data file indicates she is a dredge and pipe laying research vessel (DEX). She maintains an eight hour radio watch (H8) and has surface radar (R), radiotelephone at 2182 kHz (T), VHF-FM at 156.8 MHz (V), medium frequency at 405-535 kHz (X), high frequency at 4000-25110 kHz (Z),

(continued...)

Diverting *Discoverer*

The assignment of a surface ship to the search and rescue effort was initiated even while the MAC overflight was still being arranged. The AMVER surface picture clearly called for diverting *Discoverer* to the Mayday site.

At seven in the evening the radioman aboard *Discoverer* was sending the latest AMVER update to the Coast Guard. His transmission was interrupted by the receiving station, which requested that *Discoverer* immediately respond to a Mayday by coming to course 043 and steaming at full speed toward position 0°50'N 164°35'W. The order was passed to the bridge and noted later in the Chief Scientist's Cruise Report:

> "During Leg IV, at 0600 GMT April 22, upon departing station at 4°S 170°W, *Discoverer* was requested by USCG Rescue Coordination Center to assist the sailing vessel *Haleakala*, reported sinking with one person aboard about 420 nm to the northeast."

As *Discoverer* came to the new course, the engine room was requested to provide maximum sustainable speed. This was an

---

[60](...continued)
and single side-band (S) radio communication capabilities. She is currently at 5 degrees south and 170 degrees west proceeding north (000.0) at 14 knots having just gotten underway from her last research station (OPAREA).

emergency call for extraordinary speed and implied "red-lining" the engines.[61]

With the call for maximum speed, all four Diesel electric generators were brought on-line and throttled up to the point where they began to overheat.[62] When the oil temperature on any of the Diesel engines reached the "red-line," that engine, alone, would be throttled down just enough so the oil temperature would drop below the red-line and then it would again be throttled up. In this way *Discoverer* was able to make about 17 knots instead of the normal 14 knots as entered in AMVER or the 15 knots maximum rated cruising speed.

Now assigned to a SAR mission being coordinated by the JRCC, *Discoverer* began a series of reports, first to COMMSTA who had diverted her, and subsequently directly to the JRCC. The first report was relayed from COMMSTA to the JRCC and appears below as Document 5.

One half hour later the JRCC in Honolulu sent the details of the SAR mission to the *Discoverer* by a copy of its first

---

[61]A Diesel electric system is used to power the twelve foot twin propellers of the ship. Each prop is connected to its own 2,500 horse power DC electric motor. The two motors receive power from four 1,150 Kw Diesel electric generators. These generators can be connected to the motors in various configurations so that from one to four generators can be used to power the twin screws. Typically only two or three generators would be used to maintain cruising speed while the fourth would be taken off-line for maintenance.

[62]While the engine room is normally an uncomfortably hot place to work, deliberate overheating of the engines made the engine room of *Discoverer* more unbearable than usual and the engine room crew had to take additional breaks to cool off.

Document 5.
22 APR 0651Z (2050W) 8:50 p.m. Telex.

FROM COGARD COMMSTA HONOLULU HI
TO JRCC HONOLULU HI

THE FOLLOWING WAS RECEIVED FROM THE NOAA
DISCOVERER AT 22 APR 0644Z.

QUOTE

1. POSITION AT 22 APR 0619Z IS 03-47S 170-00.2W.
PROCEEDING ON COURSE 049 TRUE AT 17 KNOTS.
WOULD ARRIVE ON SCENE AT 23 APR 0719Z.

2. REQUEST OF NOAA MARINE OPERATOR IN SEATTLE
WASHINGTON INFORMATION ON ANY TRAFFIC.

UNQUOTE

Distress Situation Report on *Haleakala*. The report included: a description of the situation and vessel, the actions that had been taken, and the future steps that were intended. Although the vessel colors had been described to the JRCC as pale yellow with brown trim, the vessel description which follows refers to: "... white pontoons painted dark red below ...." While "pontoons" is a common misnomer for the "hulls" of a multi-hull, the dark red color below the water line was stressed because it could be assumed that the vessel was upside-down making the dark red of the bottom paint the most visible part of the boat although dark red is very hard to see against deep blue ocean water.

This message also contained the formal requests for SAR forces including the request for *Discoverer* to divert to the last known position of *Haleakala* for search and rescue.

102

Document 6.
22 APR 0731Z (2131W) 9:31 p.m. Telex (page 1 of 2).

FROM JRCC HONOLULU HI
TO <The Coast Guard Commandant Washington, DC, with
copies to the NOAA ship *Discoverer*, NOAA Marine Operations,
and 13 Air Force bases and Coast Guard stations.>

SUBJECT: DISTRESS SITUATION REPORT NUMBER ONE
    RE. SAILING VESSEL HALEAKALA TAKING ON WATER.

1. SITUATION:

    A.   22 APR 0319Z RECEIVED REPORT VIA LOCAL HAM
    OPERATOR OF THE SAILING VESSEL HALEAKALA
    TAKING ON WATER. SATNAV POSITION 00-50.04N
    164-35.04W, APPROXIMATELY 360 NAUTICAL MILES
    FROM CHRISTMAS ISLAND.

    B.   VESSEL DESCRIPTION: 56 FOOT TWIN HULLED
    CATAMARAN, US DOCUMENTATION NUMBER 597 789
    WITH WHITE PONTOONS PAINTED DARK RED BELOW
    THE WATER LINE. VESSEL HAS ONE PERSON ON
    BOARD, FLARES, SIGNALING DEVICES, EPIRB/ELT
    TURNED ON AND TRANSMITTING ON 121.5 MHZ.
    VESSEL HAS DINGHY BUT NO LIFE RAFT ON BOARD.
    WIFE CALLED AND CONFIRMED HER HUSBAND'S TRIP
    TO HONOLULU. OPERATOR IS AN EXPERIENCED
    SAILOR TRAINED IN SURVIVAL TECHNIQUES. VESSEL
    IS A BACK YARD BUILT BOAT CONSTRUCTED OF
    WOOD AND FIBERGLASS OVERLAY WITH THREE INCH
    FOAM CORE IN THE WING. ADDITIONAL LAND LINE
    CHECKS ON VESSEL CONFIRM ITINERARY.

In addition to the four formal requests for SAR forces
detailed in the wire, the JRCC was also checking for the
availability of patrol planes from the 6594th TEST Group at

Document 7.
22 APR 0731Z (2131W) 9:31 p.m. Telex (page 2 of 2).

2. ACTIONS:

A.   22 APR 0400Z VESSEL DID NOT COME UP ON SCHEDULED COMMUNICATIONS CHECK.

B.   22 APR 0420Z DIVERTED AIR PACIFIC FLIGHT 551 TO OVERFLY POSITION AND CONFIRM EPIRB/ELT TRANSMITTING. ESTIMATED TIME OF ARRIVAL OF FLIGHT 551 ON STATION IS 22 APR 0600Z.

3. INTENTIONS:

A.   FOR PACIFIC AIRLIFT COMMAND CENTER:
REQUEST SUITABLE AIRCRAFT FOR ELECTRONIC AND FLARE SEARCH AND POSSIBLE AIR DROP OF LIFE RAFT PRIOR TO THE EARLIEST POSSIBLE ARRIVAL OF A COAST GUARD AIRCRAFT ON STATION.

B. FOR AIR STATION BARBERS POINT:
COAST GUARD C-130, FLIGHT NUMBER CG-1414 WILL DEPART 22 APR 1200Z FOR CHRISTMAS ISLAND. CG-1414 WILL STAGE FROM CHRISTMAS ISLAND AND BEGIN SEARCHING BY THE FIRST LIGHT OF DAWN.

C. FOR NOAA SHIP DISCOVERER:
REQUEST DIVERT TO VESSELS LAST KNOWN POSITION FOR SEARCH AND RESCUE. NO OTHER VESSELS WITHIN 900 NAUTICAL MILES OF POSITION.

D. FOR 41ST RESCUE & WEATHER RECONNAISSANCE WING, MCCLELLAN AIR FORCE BASE, CALIFORNIA:
REQUEST SUITABLE AIRCRAFT TO STAGE OUT OF CHRISTMAS ISLAND FOR DAYLIGHT SEARCH BEGINNING 22 APRIL AND EXTENDING ANY ADDITIONAL DAYS IT IS AVAILABLE.

Hickam and the 22nd Group at Travis through PALCC. The last formal request for an aircraft to be assigned to the SAR mission by McClellan Air Force Base in California was an indication of just how difficult[63] locating three patrol planes had become.

Referring to the surface picture table and plot in the previous chapter, *Discoverer*, vessel number six, was clearly the closest ship in both distance and time being only 34 cruising hours from *Haleakala* and 475 nautical miles away. However, the wire went on to inform *Discoverer* there were no other vessels within 900 nautical miles of *Haleakala*. The implications of this statement were quite correct although, in fact, one other ship, vessel number four, was within 800 miles and three ships, numbers one, four, and five were within the 900 miles. Nevertheless, the second closest vessel in terms of cruising time to *Haleakala* was *Columbus Queensland*, ship number three, 50 hours and 927 nautical miles away. Although farther than the 900 miles away, her faster speed made her the second choice to search for *Haleakala*. Therefore, the second closest ship (in terms of arrival time) was over 900 miles away.

By a quarter to ten, *Discoverer* had been underway toward the Mayday site for more than two and a half hours. An hourly report to the JRCC stated she was proceeding to assist at her fastest possible speed. However, her speed had actually dropped from 17 to 15 knots, possibly due to having taken one of the Diesel generators off-line for maintenance. A new estimate of arrival on station at the search area was reported as 23 APR

---

[63]This problem in locating aircraft had not yet been relayed to Elli.

1000Z,[64] along with a note that this eleven p.m. arrival will be in darkness at the Mayday site.

Discoverer also updated the AMVER SAR database to include radio direction finding (RDF) capability for all frequencies in the range of 200 kHz to 13.8 MHz, on both AM and SSB, while communication capability covered 2 to 30 MHz. Note that both reception and RDF for the 121.5 and 243 MHz emergency frequencies of the EPIRB were <u>not</u> available aboard the assigned rescue vessel.[65]

The deck officers had been studying charts of the Mayday site. The pilot charts show a 1 knot westward drift for the position given for *Haleakala* and it would take also 31 hours to get to the site. Therefore, they requested JRCC to consider diverting *Discoverer* to a point 31 miles west of the JRCC assigned destination—00°50.04'N 164°35.04'W. In addition they asked the JRCC to advise them of all subsequent SAR information such as the outcome of the Flight 551 overflight.

22 APR 0900Z (2200X): 03°18.2'S 169°27.5'W, 10:00 p.m.

By ten o'clock the speed had gone back up half a knot to 15.5 knots. JRCC had not yet responded to the request for course change, and the ship was still in route to 00°50'N

---

[64]The speed reduction added over two and a half hours to the expected arrival time.

[65]*Discoverer* also had communication capability via the old ATS-1 single channel, geosynchronous communications satellite although it was not noted in this message.

164°35'W for Search and Rescue within a 50 nautical mile area of the Mayday site.

22 APR 1100Z (0000X): 02°59.6'S 169°08.7'W, Midnight.

At midnight the *Discoverer* was at 02°59.6'S 169°08.7'W and the course was still 050. Phoenix Island lay 109 nautical miles away on a bearing of 246 degrees True.

Although still showing over 15 knots through the water, the actual average speed over the ground[66] was nearer 13 knots as calculated based on the change in position of the vessel in the preceding two hours.

By five in the morning the JRCC had agreed to order a course change. The new course was 049, the new destination 00°34.0'N 165°27.0'W.[67]

---

[66]The speed of a vessel is measured in two different ways: the speed of the boat through the water, which corresponds to how fast the water is rushing by the vessel; and the boat speed over the ground, which refers to the speed over the land under the water under the boat, the ocean bottom in this case. Speed over the ground, also referred to as the speed made good, thus accounts for the water current.

[67]*Discoverer* had requested consideration of a destination 0 nautical miles south and 31 nautical miles west of the reported position while the new destination was 16 nautical miles south and 7 nautical miles west of the position. The JRCC had used the assumed drift direction and speed to calculate an estimated position for *Haleakala* to be at the expected time of arrival of Discoverer. The drift direction and speed would have been calculated assuming that the wind was the major driving force.

The destination suggested by *Discoverer* was based on the current only -- which, at the Mayday site, flows to the west at just under one knot. Hence a diversion of 31 miles was requested for the expected position in the 31 hours it would take to arrive on scene.

Search Plans

I had been out of radio contact since the capsize and knew nothing of the search plans being formulated as the evening wore on in Honolulu. Nor did I know that Flight 551 had reported "No Joy"[68] at hearing no EPIRB signal on the overflight. By late evening MAC-38084 was airborne and en route.

22 APR 0735Z (2135W) 9:35 p.m.

The US Air Force 6594th Group reported to the JRCC that they would also support the SAR mission with a patrol plane. They estimated ten o'clock the next morning would be the soonest[69] they could have the search plane ready to takeoff from Hickam.

The 6594th also wanted to know if they would still be needed on Monday. If so, the sooner the request for the aircraft was made, the earlier they would be able to have the plane ready to depart from Hickam on Monday. The Air Force commander

---

[68]"No Joy" is a common euphemism used by the Coast Guard and others for "failure" of a search mission objective, apparently because the broadcast of the word "failure" might evoke unduly strong emotions in the listener, particularly if the listener is one who is emotionally involved with the mission.

"Joy" is similar jargon for "success."

[69]If it left by ten it should arrive at the equator to begin searching by two-thirty in the afternoon. The plane would be able to continue searching until dark and then return to Hickam although it would be near its maximum endurance aloft.

stated he did not want the plane to stage from Christmas Island because no mechanical service for the aircraft was available there.

MAC-38084 was nearly half way between Pago Pago and the Mayday site when the JRCC recorded the Mayday situation assessment in the SAR case log.

Document 8.
22 APR 0900Z (2300W) 11:00 p.m. Situation assessment.

```
2300W    ASSUMPTIONS FOR CAPSIZED VESSEL
         PROBABILITY SUNK 50% PROBABILITY AWASH 50%
         PERSON IN WATER ATTACHED TO FLOTSAM WITH
         ELT/EPIRB ACTIVATED.  SEA CURRENT 0.6 KNOTS
```

These Mayday situation assumptions by the JRCC were reasonable, well thought out, and consistent with the established guidelines. Nevertheless, they had a certain degree of inaccuracy.[70]

---

[70] The most important fact (to me) about the situation assessment was that it was accepted that there was a genuine Mayday emergency aboard *Haleakala* as reported. (Note how valuable independent verification is to establish a Mayday mission.)

The JRCC concluded *Haleakala* had certainly capsized with a fifty percent probability that the vessel had then sunk. This conclusion was erroneous because of the fact that multihulls normally cannot sink and additional assurance had been given by me and by Elli that *Haleakala* had no ballast and would continue to float even upside down.

The conclusion that there was a the survivor attached to flotsam was a quite reasonable assumption and I would have been in this situation if the boat broke-up. The EPIRB/ELT should have been activated and I should have kept

(continued...)

22 APR 1000Z (0000W) Midnight.

The launch of the SAR forces officially began a few minutes after midnight, Sunday morning in Honolulu, although both MAC-38084 and *Discoverer* were already in route to the site, and CG-1414 was being readied for the flight to arrive at Christmas at dawn. (See Document 7.)

22 APR 1112Z (0112W) 1:12 a.m.

Having been informed that the 6594th had a patrol plane available, the JRCC officially requested that this search aircraft be assigned from Hickam Air Force Base for locating the distressed vessel 360 nautical miles west of Christmas Island.

By the wee hours of the morning the JRCC had completed the initial search plan. The first overflight search of area A-1 by Flight 551 was unsuccessful. Details of the second search plan were reported to the rescue forces in the early morning wire reproduced starting with document Document 9. below.

Note that the weather was reported to be scattered thunder storms with showers, with the same forecast for the next two days.

---

[70](...continued)
the radio with me at all costs.

Finally, the SAR assumption that the sea current was carrying all the flotsam and survivor, if any, toward the west at 0.6 knots was based on well founded experience. Although this assumption was nearly correct, the data on which it must have been based should have predicted figure about three or four times larger and the surface current should have been west southwest instead of west.

Document 9.
22 APR 1328Z (0328W) 3:28 a.m. Telex (page 1 of 4).

FROM JRCC HONOLULU HI
TO <The Coast Guard, Air Force, and NOAA rescue forces
    and their respective parent command centers>
SUBJECT: SAILING VESSEL HALEAKALA TAKING ON
WATER.

1. SITUATION:

A. 22 APR 0319Z RECEIVED REPORT VIA LOCAL HAM
OPERATOR OF THE SAILING VESSEL HALEAKALA
TAKING ON WATER. SATNAV POSITION 00-50.04N
164-35.04W, APPROXIMATELY 360 NAUTICAL MILES
FROM CHRISTMAS ISLAND.

B. VESSEL DESCRIPTION: 56 FOOT TWIN HULLED
CATAMARAN, US DOCUMENTATION NUMBER 597 789
WITH WHITE HULLS PAINTED DARK RED BELOW THE
WATER LINE. VESSEL HAS ONE PERSON ON BOARD,
FLARES, SIGNALING DEVICES, EPIRB/ELT TURNED ON
AND TRANSMITTING ON 121.5 MHZ. VESSEL HAS
DINGHY BUT NO LIFE RAFT ON BOARD.

C. WEATHER FORECAST FOR MAYDAY SITE:
SCATTERED THUNDER STORMS WITH SHOWERS,
BROKEN AND OVERCAST SKY, WIND FROM THE EAST
NORTHEAST AT 8 TO 15 KNOTS, WITH GUSTS OF 20 TO
30 KNOTS IN STORMS, SEAS FROM THE EAST
NORTHEAST 4 TO 7 FEET WITH A PERIOD OF 7
SECONDS. SAME FORECAST IS VALID FOR THE NEXT
48 HOURS.

The search plan defines the details of the four overlapping search areas (B-1 through B-4) and the planned search pattern within each area. The ship wreckage is assumed to be drifting in the "creep" direction of 245 degrees at 0.6 knots.

Document 10.
22 APR 1328Z (0328W) 3:28 a.m. Telex (page 2 of 4).

2. SEARCH AREA:

AREA	SIZE	AXIS	CORNER POINTS	ALTITUDE
B-1	6400 SQNM	245	01-08N 165-34W	2000 FT
			01-42N 164-19W	
			00-30N 163-45W	
			00-04S 164-59W	
B-2	7200 SQNM	245	01-08N 165-54W	500 FT
			01-42N 164-34W	
			00-30N 164-00W	
			00-08S 165-21W	
B-3	1600 SQNM	245	00-42N 165-53W	1000 FT
			01-00N 165-18W	
			00-24N 165-02W	
			00-07N 165-37W	
B-4	900 SQNM	245	00-34N 165-27W	SURFACE

3. EXECUTION:

AREA	UNIT	C/S	PATTERN	CREEP	COMMENCE SEARCH POINT
B-1	MAC 38084		SS	245	00-50.04N 164-35.00W
B-2	CG 1414		PS	245	01-08N 165-54W
B-3	AFR 823		PS	245	00-42N 165-53W
B-4	DISCOVERER		SS	245	00-34N 165-27W

Document 11.
22 APR 1328Z (0328W) 3:28 a.m. Telex (page 3 of 4).

---

4. COORDINATING INSTRUCTIONS:

   A. JRCC DESIGNATED SAR MISSION COORDINATOR

   B. CG 1414 DESIGNATED ON SCENE COMMANDER

   C. AIRBORNE AND SURFACE UNIT ARRIVAL TIMES:
   MAC 38084   ON THE SCENE AT 22 APR 1220Z
   CG 1414   ON THE SCENE AT 22 APR 1800Z
   AFR 823   ON THE SCENE AT 23 APR 0230Z
   DISCOVERER   ON THE SCENE AT 23 APR 0730Z

   D. MINIMUM 78 PERCENT PROBABILITY OF DETECTION
   DESIRED AND/OR DESIRED TRACK SPACING 4
   NAUTICAL MILES. REDUCE TRACK SPACING TO 1
   NAUTICAL MILE IF WEATHER PERMITS. TRACK
   SPACING FOR B-4 IS 1 NAUTICAL MILE.

   E. ON SCENE COMMANDER AUTHORIZED TO ALTER
   SEARCH PLAN AS SITUATION DICTATES. ADVISE SAR
   MISSION COORDINATOR OF CHANGES TO ON SCENE
   WEATHER AND ANY OTHER SIGNIFICANT
   INFORMATION.

5. COMMUNICATIONS:
   PRIMARY: 5696.0 KHZ,
   SECONDARY: 381.8 MHZ,
   TERTIARY: 8984.0 KHZ, OR
                 123.1 MHZ.

The overlapping pattern of the proposed searches is plotted in Figure 10 using the data from Document 9., Document 10.

113

Document 12.

22 APR 1328Z (0328W) 3:28 a.m. Telex (page 4 of 4).

---

6. REPORTS:

A. ON SCENE COMMANDER SEND SITUATION
REPORTS UPON ARRIVAL ON STATION AND EVERY 4
HOURS TO INCLUDE THE WEATHER.

B. AT THE END DAY OPERATIONS, PARENT COMMAND
TO REPORT SORTIES, HOURS FLOWN, AREA
SEARCHED, PROBABILITY OF DETECTION ATTAINED,
AND ANY DEVIATIONS ON SEARCH PLAN TO SAR
MISSION COORDINATOR.

The wreckage symbol is plotted at the reported position of *Haleakala*.[71] The two areas B-1 and B-4 are to be searched with a square search pattern (SS) starting at the Commence Search Points (CSP) plotted, while areas B-2 and B-3 are to be searched in parallel search patterns (PS).[72] Both a four nautical mile circle and a one nautical mile circle are plotted to scale to illustrate the limited visual range of the search craft. At two thousand feet altitude and four nautical mile track spacing, the search by MAC-38084 is expected to have only a 78 percent

---

[71]The area covered by Figure 10 is shown by the dotted square in Figure 9 on page 98.

[72]A square search pattern consists of a series of expanding squares where each succeeding square is larger than the proceeding by one track spacing as illustrated at the CSP for B-4.

A parallel search pattern consists of a series of parallel lines separated from each other by the track spacing as illustrated at the CSP of area B-2.

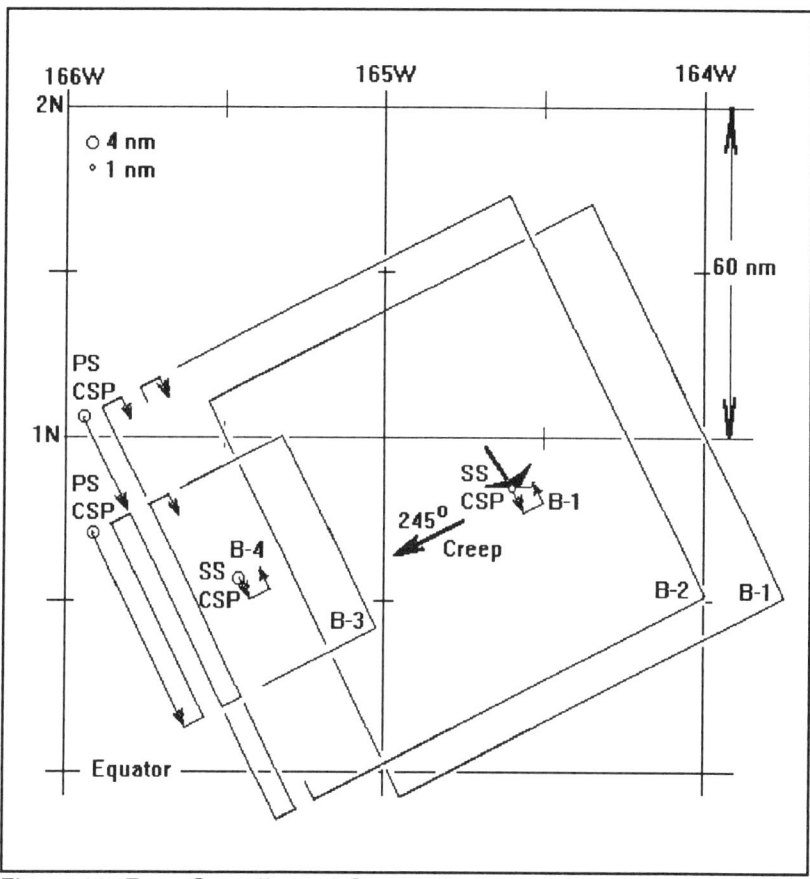

Figure 10 **Four Coordinated Search Patterns.**

chance of spotting the wreckage. That is, there is nearly a one in four chance they would miss seeing any wreckage even if they flew over the spot in the designated pattern. The multiple search patterns by different craft are used to increase the probability of spotting the wreckage providing it is <u>in fact</u> in the designated area.

115

I would have been elated to know that there was going to be even an attempt at the limited search and rescue which I was hoping for and ecstatic if I had known a multi-phase formal search and rescue plan was being developed.

A Star Moved

I knew it was approaching midnight as I watched my Orion clock setting on the horizon, when I saw a flicker of movement. A star moved in Orion! My spirits soared. Maybe the Coast Guard had been able to get me help in only a matter of hours instead of a number of days as I had more realistically expected. But before I let myself get too excited I wanted to be sure I had not seen a mirage. There were scattered rain squall clouds nearby still partially obscuring the horizon, and I stared at the moving star among the clouds to be absolutely certain it actually HAD moved. Yes it was moving! "Sadie, we're saved!"

If it was a plane I had to get their attention immediately. If it was not the Coast Guard, they might not be looking for anyone and could just fly by me. It had happened to others many times before, even after survivors had "wasted" several flares trying to attract attention of the airplane or ship.

The flare gun was still on the long lanyard around my neck and tucked into my pocket. I yanked it out, quickly loaded it, cocked the hammer, pointed it up, and fired a bright red flare into the air. I immediately reloaded the flare gun to be ready for another shot.

It looked like the lights of a plane at low altitude several miles away, although it could still be a ship. I was really excited because I was now becoming convinced that it was a plane due west in the constellation Orion at the horizon and that the plane was searching for me. They should have expected me to be in that direction due to the strong equatorial current. However, since I was "sailing" toward the wind I was east of where they should expect me to be. This was more convincing evidence that they were looking for me and were not just a passing airplane. They might be able to rescue me![73]

I climbed up on the keel, and held up the large strobe as high as I could while I watched the moving star. I had the flare gun in the other hand ready to fire a second flare in a couple of more minutes. The "star" stopped moving, and I was certain it was a rescue airplane heading my way.

The light got brighter and brighter and the dark shape of an airplane appeared behind the bright lights. I tucked the flare gun back in my pocket and turned on the flashlight. I now held my arms straight out to the side. In one hand I still held the large strobe and in the other I held the flashlight pointed at the plane. I was thrilled as the plane, jet engines screaming, flew directly over my head. Even as they flew over they kept a bright light trained on me.

---

[73]This was a quite optimistic although also quite unrealistic thought.

Although I could not make out any of its details, I could tell the airplane was a large jet.[74] The airplane had flown low over me at an altitude of a couple of hundred feet, and was now banking to the left, making what seemed to be a rather tight circle for such a large jet. Then it flew back over me a second time. On the third pass I heard a Whomp! Whomp! It sounded like they were dropping someone or something in the water. In the dark I could not tell what it was.

The object(s) splashed into the sea ahead and to the right of the boat. I thought paramedics might have parachuted into the water, remembering the scuba equipped paramedics who were dropped in the water to go to the astronauts after an ocean splash-down.[75]

I blew my whistle and shouted to the shapes in the water hoping I had human company. There was no answer, no sound. In a few minutes, by the lights of the passing plane, I could see that one of the things was a raft, and I assumed that they also had dropped me supplies. The raft was a long distance off, perhaps two or three hundred yards. It was floating by rather rapidly as we moved ahead and the wind blew it past. There

---

[74]I found out later it was a C-141 painted a dark, dull, olive drab camouflage color. The camouflage finish was effective in hiding its identity from me, and I could see no markings. On the other hand, I must have been quite visible to them. They had strong search lights, probably landing lights under the wings, which they pointed down as they passed over.

[75]I later learned that Search and Rescue does not include suicide missions. If a rescue ship was on the scene or nearly so, and there was an immediate life threatening medical problem below, they might ask for volunteers. Neither criteria was true in my case, and no such drop would have been allowed by the very sensible regulations.

was clearly no point in trying to get to it, it was much too far away, so I just ignored it.

The plane continued to circle.

The back doors of the lighted plane were open, and I could see people inside as they again flew over. Whomp! There was another drop. I figured that the sound might be made by an opening parachute. This time the drop was a lot closer. In the glare of the floodlights from the cargo bay, I now could see another raft had been dropped. This raft seemed to inflate as it left the plane and tumbled to the ocean.

After the raft hit the water I could see it was going to drift by much closer, about seventy-five yards away. I had to immediately make up my mind whether to go for this raft or to stay with the boat. I only had a few seconds before the new raft would also pass by and become too far away to swim to. I also wanted to save Sadie and I knew she wouldn't be able to swim alongside as I swam for the raft. I had to quickly evaluate the pros and cons and make the life or death decision to stay where I was or go for the raft. Obviously they wanted me to swim to the raft they had dropped.

Drifting Wreckage

MAC-38084 had been on a routine flight ferrying military passengers and cargo before it was diverted to search for the drifting wreckage of *Haleakala*. Although all military crews are trained in survival functions, such a search and rescue assignment is unusual, and MAC-38084 did not have the equipment or practice that would be expected of a full time SAR unit with a primary responsibility for search and rescue. The SAR assignment was to attempt to locate *Haleakala* near 00°50'N 164°35'W using both a flare search and an RDF search for an EPIRB operating on 121.5 and 243 Mhz. Once having located the vessel they were to be prepared to drop a life raft prior to the earliest possible arrival of a Coast Guard patrol plane.

MAC-38084 had been instructed to use an expanding square search pattern of the B-1 area[76] as shown in Figure 11. This figure graphically illustrates some of the possible confusion that can arise in any remotely directed operation and especially when a commandeered unit is being deployed.[77]

---

[76]The search should be conducted as follows:

1) Fly to the Commence Search Point, the center of the assigned Expanding Square Search Area.

2) Turn to line-up with the creep angle, here ENE.

3) Fly one half of the track separation, here 2 nautical miles and turn 90-degrees to the right.

4) Fly pairs of search legs each leg ending with a 90-degree right turn and the pair being first one times the track separation distance (or 4 nautical miles) then two times the track separation, then three ....

[77]Where should the search begin, that is, where is the Search Commencement Point? Initially the CSP is at the know position, the 0240 Fix. However the CSP should move in the calculated creep direction. Thus it should be at the plotted 1045Z estimated position (EP) for the estimated time of arrival of the search aircraft. On the other hand, if the direction and/or magnitude of the creep is uncertain, then the original CSP based on the fix rather than the later estimated position should be used.

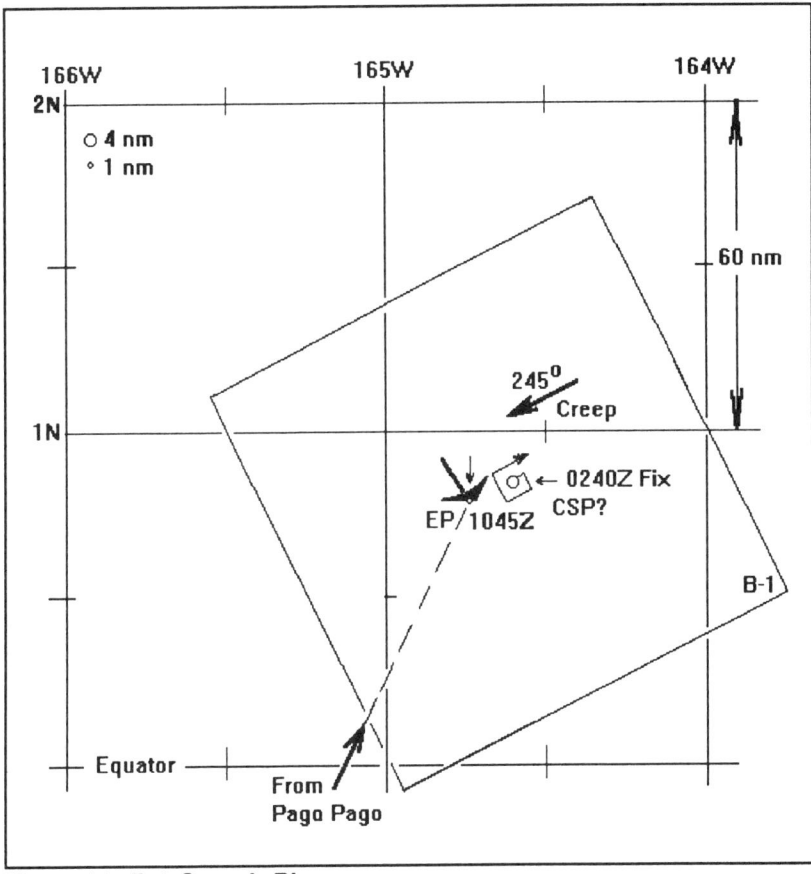

Figure 11 **B-1 Search Plan.**

The two most probable courses[78] for the MAC-38084 approach flight to have taken are plotted in Figure 12. They are the course from Pago Pago to the last reported position of *Haleakala*, the 0240Z fix, and to the 1045Z estimated (expected)

---

[78]The flight may have been in constant radio contact with the JRCC but no records of the in-flight conversations remain. The exact course of the flight and target destination are lost to the record.

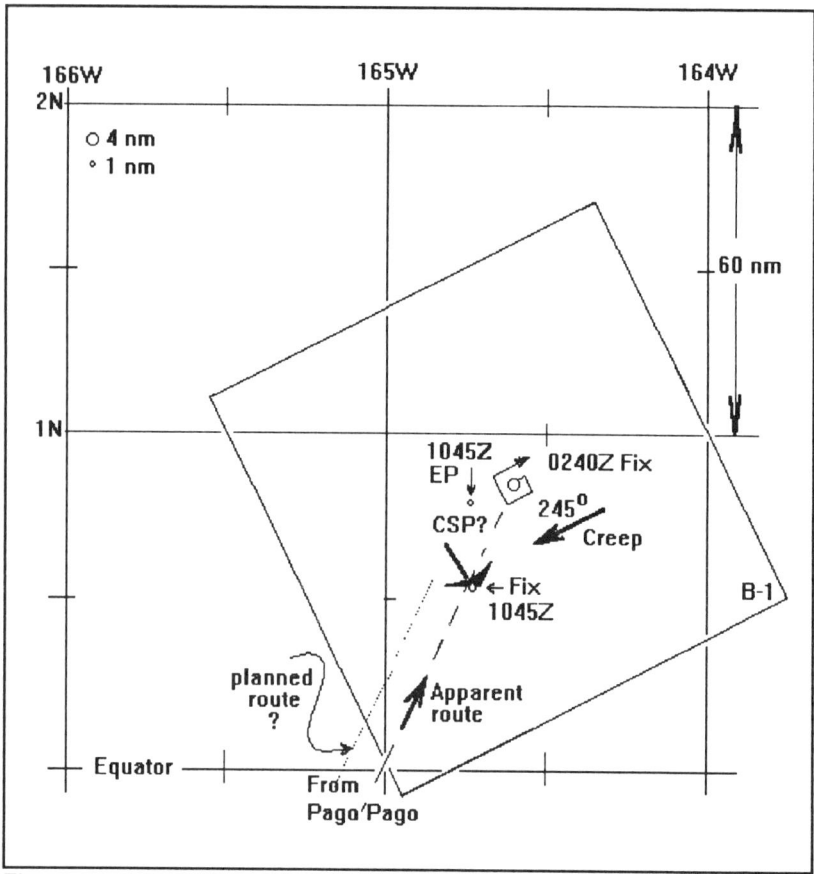

Figure 12 **MAC-38084 Search.**

position (EP) eight miles to the west. Whichever course was flown, I apparently saw the plane as it flew by and diverted it with a flare before it reached the actual assigned commence search point (CSP).

122

22 APR 1045Z (2345X) 00°34.10'N 164°43.7'W, 11:45 p.m. Flare.

When MAC-38084 saw the flare just before midnight, flew over the site, and logged its position, they had successfully accomplished the initial phase of the SAR mission. They had located the drifting wreckage and made visual contact with a survivor.

The view of the situation from the airplane aloft and from my vantage at sea level were quite different. The critical missing element was effective communication between us. This lack of mutual understanding led to some immediate problems, and these problems compounded as events unfolded. My most pressing problem was for survival supplies, while my greatest contribution to later recovery might have been the explanation I could offer as to why I was not at the expected position.[79]

Lure of the Raft

The second raft the plane dropped was irresistible. The lure of the raft was for the survival supplies. Since *Haleakala* could not sink out from under me and was now a raft itself, the

---

[79]Because I was unable to communicate my understanding of the situation at this point in the story, I will defer further explanation and my reasoning as to why I was not where they could have expected to find me. Further detailed analysis appears in the last chapter at the point where it came up again in discussions with the SAR center personnel.

123

flotation aspect of the inflatable raft was not a factor in my decision.

Of the supplies I missed most of all, foremost was my EPIRB. I had left it in its bracket in the main cabin before the capsize. It was now two feet below the surface and probably shorted because the antenna was submerged, but it might still work if and when I could retrieve it. But, it also may have been damaged or fallen out of its bracket and simply gone into the deep six.

All the supplies inside *Haleakala* were equally difficult or impossible to access in the overturned and submerged cabin. The dropped raft promised the survival gear I desperately needed. I realized that rescue might take considerable time in this remote spot and that I would need provisions and supplies to keep me until then. And lastly, since they had now dropped two rafts for me they must think that it would be better for me to be aboard one of the rafts than where I was. Since I had stressed to the Coast Guard the fact that *Haleakala* could not sink, I assumed they knew I did not need a rescue platform but needed emergency supplies.

There was no more time to weigh the odds. I had to make up my mind now, instantly.

I decided to go for it.

I grabbed Sadie and put her on the back of my life jacket as I had done after the capsize, slipped down into the water, and started swimming for the raft. It was drifting by at a fast clip[80] and was probably fifty yards away when I started for it.

When I reached it I found a very large inflated raft, large enough to hold more than a dozen people. It was a bright orange and had a light. It was too big to climb into out of the water. But I quickly discovered that it also had several ramps built into the sides with handrails so a person could pull himself up out of the water and on to the raft.

When I first caught hold of the raft, I took Sadie off the back of my life Jacket, set her up on the ramp, and gave her a little push so she would go aboard. Then I grabbed the handrails and pulled myself up the ramp and into the raft.

I just lay there a few moments catching my breath. My all-out dash had left me panting. After a few moments I started to breathe easier and took off some of my burdensome equipment. I set my flare gun down in the middle of the floor along with some of the spare flares out of my pocket. It now was clear this raft was going to be our home for awhile.

Now that we were safely aboard the life raft, it was time to locate the survival supplies. I really hoped to find a radio to be able to talk to the airplane still circling above. But a rapid search all around the large raft with my flashlight, plus the light from the plane as it passed, showed nothing. There was nothing at all visible in the raft! Not even a canopy for shade from the sun! Surely the rescue plane had not dropped an empty life raft without supplies!

---

[80]The relative speed of the raft was partly due to the fact that we were going east northeast while it was drifting west southwest.

A second more careful search of the entire raft was equally unsuccessful. There was no list of contents or survival advice which I expected to see printed on the inside of the raft. At the very least I expected to find identification, such as "US Coast Guard" and brief instructions, perhaps in several languages. But nothing came to light in my frantic search.

Amazed and somewhat angry, I could not believe that all Sadie and I had been given to survive was an empty orange raft. Then I spotted a line going down into the water. My spirits rose as I grabbed for it; whatever was tied to the line may have fallen out as the raft tumbled from the airplane.

I quickly pulled in on the line to find only a drogue (sea anchor) at the very end. I put the drogue back out to limit the drift of the raft and sat down on the floor to decide what to do next.

Full of questions, I looked up at the patrolling plane:

"Do you know that there are no supplies on this raft?"

"Were you able to see me well enough flying back and forth overhead to realize I was searching the raft but have not found the supplies I need?"

"Are survival supplies normally dropped separately?"

"Could there be a survival package floating in the water somewhere?"

"Did they first wait for me to get to the raft and, seeing that I have made it aboard, will now drop supplies?"

As if they had read my mind, something else dropped from the plane on the next pass. I could see it in the distance, but it was too dark to make out what kind of object had been dropped.

However, this new thing had a striking flashing strobe to catch my attention and seemed close enough to consider another swim. I felt that I could swim to it and back without getting separated from Sadie. I turned on my flashlight and put it down in the raft to comfort her. Then I slid over the side into the water and took hold of the line that went out to the drogue. I pulled in and collapsed the drogue. Then, holding the drogue line as a painter,[81] I swam out toward the unknown dark floating object.

When I had reached the end of the line I could see that the dark shape was another raft but it was still too far for me to reach. I began swimming very hard dragging our raft with one hand as I attempted to tow it over to the second one. I planned to lash the two together as soon as I got a hold of the other one. But towing such a big raft was slow going, and I seemed to be making no headway swimming with only one arm. I stopped to wrap the line around me to free both arms for swimming.

Using both arms now, I began swimming as hard as I could and continued to kept up the pace until I was quite winded. Gasping for breath and still making no noticeable progress, I finally stopped struggling to reconsider my alternatives. I had to make a decision whether to abandon the supplies I expected on the distant raft or to try to swim the round trip without holding on to the first raft.

Swimming over and back was very tempting. After all, the first raft might have been fully equipped when it left the plane but lost its contents when it hit the water. The crew on the

---

[81]The line tied to the bow of a dinghy and use to tie it up to when not in use is referred to as a "painter."

plane, seeing I had no supplies, had dropped me another raft with the supplies. There it was, tantalizingly close, maybe 100 feet away. The short additional swim did not seem too far to go for something so vital. I decided to give it a quick try and to swim back immediately if, by any chance, it too was empty.

I dropped the drogue line and swam for the other raft. Pulling myself up the now familiar ramp I quickly looked around. It was identical to the first with no instructions apparent. One small strobe was flashing brightly, but still no supplies and no supply compartment that I could locate. Another line led into the water. I quickly verified that it too was attached to another drogue. This raft also was without supplies.

With considerable anguish and anger, I thought: "They knew that I was the only person aboard an overturned unsinkable vessel. Why did they drop me two empty life rafts?"

But there was no time for recriminations. Since I had left Sadie and my flare gun on the other raft, I grabbed the little strobe, unfastened it, put it in my pocket, dove for the water, and immediately started to swim back. I could see the light from the flashlight I had left with Sadie and I kept my eye on it as I swam. When I got close to the light I saw *the light was not the light on the raft!*

Instead of my flashlight marking the raft with Sadie, I found a small incandescent light bobbing in the water attached to an inflated life vest! I considered picking up either the life vest or the light but I was wearing a full life jacket and did not need either another vest or another light. Worse than useless, they had distracted me from the raft. I wasted no more time. I carefully looked around again for the raft with Sadie feeling terrible for having lost sight of it in the moments while searching the second raft.

Then I saw the light a couple of dozen yards away and quickly swam toward it. ... Anger and hope. ... Fired up by adrenaline. ... Hard swimming. ... And then another inflated vest and light![82]

I stopped swimming, caught my breath and looked desperately all around, very carefully trying to pick out either life raft in the black water around me.

I was completely disoriented. Obviously I did not know where I was in relation to Sadie. As a matter of fact, I did not even know the direction back to the first inflated vest which I had just left. The raft with Sadie aboard had to be somewhere within a few dozen yards around me but I could not see it in the dark and choppy sea, and I did not even know in which direction to look for it.

I had lost contact with both rafts! Even worse, I had long since lost contact with the *Haleakala*. By this time Sadie, and I, and everything the plane had dropped, including the rafts and life vests, had all been swept a long way from the boat. Now I could not even see any other light to swim to!

My only hope for help was from the plane overhead. But how could they possibly spot me now that I had become a tiny

---

[82]Both vests must have been inflated aboard the plane and then dropped into the water. A number of them may have been dropped when they saw me swim toward the first raft. There are probably quite a number of such inflatable life vest aboard any large plane flying over water. However, I only saw the two that are mentioned.

dot floating in the huge black ocean, even if by some miracle they knew exactly where to look?

It now became quite clear to me that my survival could not depend on help from anyone else. Strangely, I remained calm and sane, unless serenity under these circumstances is insane.

Head Above the Sea

The plane continued to fly somewhere over me for nearly an hour while I was drifting alone, away from both the *Haleakala* and the rafts. The sound of the engines would come and go as the plane continued to fly about. Floating in the open ocean at night, with only my head above the sea, I was now almost completely undetectable by any means. I would remain very nearly invisible from the air[83] even at midday.

---

[83]In the bright sunshine of a clear day with four foot seas, the Coast Guard calculates that there is a 50/50 chance of a fully manned and trained SAR unit detecting a man floating in the water if they can pass within 150 feet of the target while flying at an altitude of 300 feet. In other words, it is equally probable that they would miss seeing the survivor even having flown that close at that low altitude.

Even under absolutely ideal conditions, with an unlimited number of the SAR units committed, with an unlimited amount of time, no such search pattern is even possible within the known technology. It would mean flying parallel adjacent search tracks spaced every 125 feet with a track-to-track accuracy of 25 feet over a search area starting at 3600 square nautical miles and increasing in size geometrically with time.

The only logically meaningful alternative is to recognize that there is an extremely low probability of an air search finding a target the size of a man's head floating in the water in mid ocean.

I still had the power to reason plus an overwhelming drive to survive. Although I had no food, water, or life raft, I did have a small amount of survival gear. I had a large strobe light emitting a blinding flash as it floated behind me on a yard long lanyard fastened to my safety harness. I had my whistle and knife on another lanyard around my neck. I had the small strobe from the second life raft in my pocket. I was still wearing a life jacket, safety harness, T-shirt, shorts, undershorts, shoes, socks, and I had a handkerchief and watch. Now, how could I save myself with these few things my only resources?

I sorely missed the flare gun and flashlight I had left on the raft with Sadie. Even though I had made sure to keep the large strobe light, leaving the raft without my flashlight was a violation of my own survival rules, and I swore never to make that mistake again, assuming I should I survive without it!

The airplane continued to circle above me in what appeared to me to be a random pattern. I tried to imagine what the crew knew and what, if anything, they could do to help me find the safety of either raft. They must have seen me leave *Haleakala* while they were lighting the ocean with blazing flood lights. If they flew over her again now they would also see I was not back aboard the capsized boat.

I was also certain they had seen me on the first raft after I had gotten aboard, because they had flown directly overhead providing light while I was searching for survival gear. They might not have seen me leave it, but now they must be able to tell I was not aboard either raft. What I most wanted them to do was fly in a narrow path directly over me and then continue on over to Sadie's raft, circle and return,[84] so their lights would show me the direction to swim.

Except for the strobe lights, the other few things I had seemed useless at the moment. I decided to use the strobes in an attempt to attract attention. I took the small strobe out of my pocket, turned it on and held it straight out to one side in one hand as I held the large strobe straight out the other way. I turned to face the moving plane, holding the two strobes spaced as far apart as I could hold them. I continued to turn so that I always faced the plane as it flew by.

As they flew over me, the two strobes would appear to remain spaced a constant five feet apart and a foot off of the water. Two strobes floating free in the ocean could not naturally maintain such a constant, level separation as seen from all angles. I hoped the crew would realize I had to have these two strobes in my hands, marking my position.

I considered moving the strobes back and forth, but moving them around or waving them would have been useless since they only gave off an instantaneous flash every second or two. The bright flash would freeze any motion. But the constant fixed separation between the strobes should be noticeable from the air and was the most visually striking thing I could figure out to do.

---

[84]This pattern turns out to be The Standard Pattern for Relocating Survivors which is in the form of a dumbbell with the plane flying back and forth over the expected position, circling at each end. From the air the position of the rafts and the overturned boat could be seen. Although the rafts were drifting from the boat, the position and drift of each could be accurately plotted from the air even at night illuminated by the plane's searchlights. If I were still alive, I had to be somewhere very close to the line between and including the rafts and the boat.

With the modification of the pattern to include all probable locations of the survivor, the flight path would have been exactly what I wanted them to do. A trained SAR unit would probably have followed this pattern.

I continued my visual image message as long as the plane was over me. Unfortunately, as I found out later, they never noticed anything unusual about the strobes in the water.

While I was trying to signal the plane with the strobes one of the squalls drifted over splattering me with a shower of warm rain. Now I was completely invisible from the air as the black cloud hung over my head. In the short time it took the cloud to move over and away the plane was no longer above me.

They had flown off away from me although I could still see the flood lights some distance away. As the air cleared they seemed to fly back in my general direction to resume random flying back and forth, but now not going directly over me. This time they seemed to be in more of a regular pattern than they had been flying before.

The crew obviously did not know where I was or even whether I was still alive. From the time they had first flown over me until I had started swimming back to the raft with Sadie, I had not noticed any pattern to the flight path. Now it seemed they were following a specific search pattern rather than random circling over me. The nature of the pattern and the speed of the plane took them rapidly away from me. The plane would be completely gone for increasingly longer periods of time probably flying further and further away from me[85] before each new

---

[85]Some confusion remains in my mind about these actions taken by MAC-38084. Scanty log entries are available because few of their actions in the next few hours were or needed to be reported to the JRCC. What meager records there were of this flight are no longer available because the Air Force does not preserve and archive these SAR files in contrast to the Coast Guard normal procedures.

(continued...)

approach. Even when it was close I could only tell it was there by the sound, having complete lost sight of it in the distance. After a few very distant passes, I could no longer hear the comforting roar of jet engines.

I decided my best action was to do absolutely nothing at all except to conserve my energy and to think of a way out of this now potentially fatal situation. Every other action would be futile and a deadly waste of needed energy. I was now acutely aware of the overwhelming odds. Because I did not know which way to swim, any random direction I chose would most likely take me deeper into danger, further decreasing my chances, rather than bringing me closer to survival. Furthermore, although I did not think of it at the time, struggling in the water can, itself, attract sharks.

It was quite reasonable to consider the possibility of shark attack, and many people have asked if I worried about sharks while floating alone in the middle of the ocean.

Clearly, I was extremely vulnerable to any such attack. Shark sightings while underway were rare, but on several occasions sharks had suddenly appeared around *Haleakala* as we were hove-to far at sea. I knew shark attack could occur at any time, and the ever present danger of a strike was the reason I always maintained a

---

[85](...continued)

When I realized the pattern of constantly circling above had changed I assumed they had returned to a search pattern. In retrospect, it doesn't seem to make sense that they resumed a predetermined search pattern when they had already located me and they were told that there was only one potential survivor.

shark lookout watch whenever I allowed the crew to go swimming at sea.[86]

But the single most important fact about a shark attack at that moment was that there was *positively nothing, whatsoever, I could do about it.*

I did not give shark attack another thought. If a shark was there, he would get me, and I hoped I would die quickly. If no shark was there, I was safe. There was no alternative and no possibility of protecting myself.

Any time spent worrying about sharks would be time taken from working on how to save myself. Any wasted time would decrease my chance of survival.

The waves continued to rise all night and were running about six to seven feet. At that height the crests would

---

[86]Many experienced skippers totally ban open water swimming and in my own experience sharks have appeared within two hours of being hove-to. This is supported by the figure, taken from the National Search and Rescue Manual (volume II) which indicates that floating in open ocean water that is below 66°F there is at best an average life expectancy of six hours due to hypothermia; over 66°F, the average life expectancy is limited by shark attack.

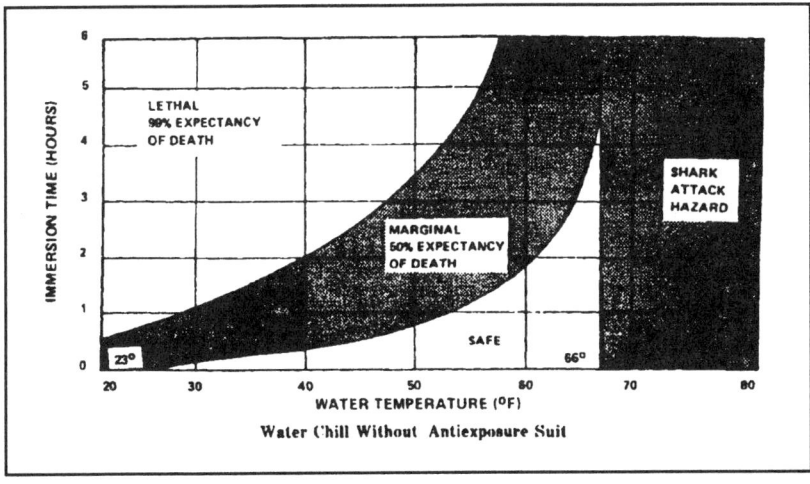

Water Chill Without Antiexposure Suit

occasionally curl off the waves, creating the sparkling white water effect of a choppy sea now visible by the phosphorescence. I usually bobbed up and down with the passing waves, but every once in a while the top of a wave would hit me in the face driving water down my nose. After I had choked on salt water a few times, I made a bridge with my hands in front of my face to block the water from entering my nose. Breathing more easily, as I floated in the water in this praying position.

In silence, alone in the black sea, completely separated from everything and everyone else in the world, I closed my eyes to the star filled sky and concentrated on my problem: "How can I possibly save myself?"

No Survivor

Although the diverted Air Pacific jetliner, Flight 551, had reported no survivor seen and no EPIRB heard, MAC-38084 had, nevertheless, continued their assignment and had flown to the disaster site. By quarter to one in the morning MAC-38084 had been on station for an hour. From aloft they had seen *Haleakala* with her hulls awash and had dropped three ten man life rafts. They had seen someone get into one of them. They reported these facts to JRCC four hours later (0445Z) adding that they had also dropped radios including an EPIRB, although I had not found any radios in the water or on the rafts at the time. MAC-38084 also observed that no transmissions, either voice or from electronic location transmitters (including the ones they had dropped), were heard after I had left the boat, except for the EPIRB still aboard *Haleakala*.[87]

Some confusion remains in my mind about the actions taken by MAC-38084 between their midnight flare sighting and their dawn report to JRCC. Scanty log entries are available because few of their actions in the next few hours were (or needed to be) reported to the JRCC. Floating in the water below, I realized the pattern of constant random circling above had changed, and I assumed they had returned to a fixed search pattern. In retrospect, it doesn't seem to make sense that they resumed a predetermined search pattern when they had already located me. Instead they should have maintained an on site, survivor sighted (and lost), flare patrol[88] until dawn.

From the air they could see the position of the rafts and the overturned boat. Although the rafts were drifting away from the boat, the position and drift of each could be accurately plotted from the air even at night by the light of the plane's searchlights. If I were still alive, I had to be somewhere very close to the line between the rafts and the overturned vessel. Although they couldn't help me directly, I would have helped myself if they had shown me the direction in which to swim. I

---

[87]Apparently no datum marker buoy was included among the radios that had been dropped with the rafts at that time. A datum marker buoy is used to mark a spot in order to be able to return to it.

[88]A flare search is one option that would have been considered by an experienced and trained SAR unit, in all probability. A parachute flare would be dropped periodically to illuminate the scene and used by the SAR unit to maintain contact with the survivor and/or wreckage.

137

could have figured out the direction to swim if they simply maintained their patrol over the rafts and wreckage.

The Coast Guard Air Station at Barbers Point had been alerted and briefed for the need for a patrol plane shortly after the SAR mission was established. The Coast Guard operates its own configuration of the C-130 Hercules from Barbers Point. Normally three planes are available for patrol. Due to mechanical trouble, only one plane could be made ready to fly by morning. Accordingly, the SAR mission was assigned to the HC-130E with call sign CG-1414.

Since the Mayday site was at the operational limit of the HC-130E, an advanced SAR staging base was considered. Christmas Island with its international airport capable of handling intercontinental jets was only 360 miles from the disaster area, and it had a communications satellite ground station. The only real problem with the use of Christmas as a SAR staging base was that the airport could not handle night traffic because it had no runway lights.

Christmas Island was contacted for the availability of jet fuel and billeting for crew relief. When the details had been arranged the Coast Guard Air Station at Barbers Point wired the American Embassy in Suva, Fiji, to arrange for official entry clearance into Christmas Island, Kiribati.[89]

---

[89]The request specifically addressed clearance for the HC-130E, call sign CG-1414, with 4 officers and 10 crew into Christmas Island, Kiribati, for fuel and crew relief. The aircraft was scheduled to depart at 22 APR 1200Z from the Naval Air Station, Barbers Point, Hawaii, and estimated to arrive at Christmas just after dawn, 6:30 a.m. local time (1630Z).

22 APR 1243Z (0243W) Barbers Point, 2:43 a.m.

As the plane left the runway, the Coast Guard Air Station at Barbers Point wired the embassy in Suva that HC-130E, CG-1414, with Lt. Siemens commanding, had departed (1242Z) for Christmas Island, Kiribati, and thence to the search area. Estimated time of arrival at Christmas was now given as 7:00 a.m. (1700Z).

22 APR 1340Z (0340W) Barbers Point, 3:40 a.m.

Less than an hour after leaving, CG-1414 had to return to Barbers Point because of continuing mechanical trouble. The new estimate of the arrival time at Christmas was now 9:00 a.m. (1900Z). The mechanics immediately resumed working on the plane. Slowly the hours went by.

More bad news came in just before seven when MAC-38084 reported that at dawn no survivor was sighted in the rafts, on the boat, or amid the debris. They called Elli to give her the latest bad news. She did not despair, clinging to the hope that I might have been able to get back inside the cabin to get out of the night weather.

CG-1414 was still on the ground with an estimate of two more hours of maintenance required. At this time the JRCC had to make a change in plans.

22 APR 1657Z (0557X) MAC-38084, 00°34.10'N 164°43.7'W, 5:57 a.m.

Although I did not see or hear them, MAC-38084 must have flown nearly over me shortly before dawn, because they reported they were on station again, and no survivor was sighted. All the life rafts, a mile and a half apart, were visible in the light of dawn, all were inflated but they reported only one had its drogue deployed. They also noted debris in the area. MAC-38084 suggested the possibility that the "owner/operator may be among the debris."

For the second time "no survivor" was reported to the JRCC. Air Pacific Flight 551 had reported "no survivor"; U.S. Air Force MAC-38084 now also reported "no survivor." The next scheduled search was to be by a Coast Guard patrol plane.

Not Despair

Adrift in mid ocean, in a most horrible and utterly desperate spot, I did not despair. Instead, I concentrated on figuring out a way to improve the chances of survival. I was still alive. And more than hope, I had the absolute determination to live. Many thoughts ran through my head as I turned my attention to the various elements of the hopeless situation:

What is my situation, what time is it, and how much time do I have?

Will I die of exposure before any possible rescue?

Where exactly am I in relation to the rafts and *Haleakala*?

Are there other rafts here in the ocean around me, or will more be dropped?

What will the Coast Guard do next to rescue me?

And the final most important question:

What questions should I be asking?

I was already shivering in the water, and I did not know the projected maximum exposure times for a person in these relatively warm seas. I was aware that fatal exposure times in icy cold water were considerably less than an hour, but that warm tropical water was not so deadly. I had snorkeled in warm water for many hours, even at night, without getting unduly chilled.

I also thought of the time I spent scuba diving in the icy waters off of Boston in the middle of winter with the protection of a wetsuit. I remembered being chilled to the bone after forty five minutes of diving even with the wetsuit and being ravenously hungry when I warmed up again.

I knew that I would certainly last until daybreak in this warm water without undue heat loss. I felt nearly as confident I could last at least another day. And my best estimate was that I could last an additional three or four days. If I could indeed stay alive that long then exposure was not the limiting factor, and I spent no more time considering hypothermia.[90]

With the danger of hypothermia ruled out, I concentrated my thoughts on locating the rafts:

The inflated rafts are mostly above the surface of the water giving them a high windage. Although they have drogues to limit their speed, this windage will make them drift rapidly. Therefore, the rafts must be traveling down-wind faster than they are being carried in the same direction by the current. The breaking action of the drogues must be designed to limit their speed to a point where a swimmer can catch up to them in heavy weather. The rafts' speed down wind should be no more than 0.2 knots and probably nearer 0.1 knot. I'll assume the speed of the rafts is 0.15 knots down wind.

My next problem was to calculate my own location, or more precisely, my drift.

In contrast to the rafts, I have very little windage because only my head and the upper part of my shoulders and life jacket are above the surface while most of my body is deep in the water. This means I am nearly still in the water, or more precisely, I must be traveling at nearly the speed of the current.

The location of *Haleakala* was easy to figure:

---

[90]In fact, by accident I had chosen the ideal place to be exposed. Survival time immersed in the tropical waters of the equator has exceeded 80 hours and is limited by dehydration and fatigue. I was in much greater danger from sharks than from hypothermia. Even though I was shivering and felt chilled, the water at the equator is too warm for one to die of exposure.

I already know that the boat was going up wind at 0.5 knots. Her last course was 080 degrees True. She will certainly remain on that course unless and until the wind changes direction.

Putting all of my calculations and estimates together, I concluded:

I left *Haleakala* at about midnight, and it will be dawn before I can search for her again. By then she will have "sailed" away from me for six hours and should be on a bearing of 080 and about three miles away (0.5 knots for 6 hours is 3 nautical miles).

I left the second orange inflated raft at about one o'clock. By dawn the rafts should be on a bearing of 260 degrees True, which is 180 degrees away from the wind, and they should be at a distance of 0.75 miles drifting at 0.15 knots for five hours.

Would I be able to see far enough and well enough without my contacts to see them in the daylight?

From my eye level of one foot above the surface of the water, I can see around me for a maximum of a hundred yards or less but, as I bob up, I get glimpses of the water much further away. I hope this upward motion will be enough to be able to see the bright orange of the rafts three quarters of a mile away to the west at dawn. I will be much closer to the rafts than to the boat, and I hope I will be close enough to see them. But I am reasonably sure that it will be impossible for me to see the boat, because she will be three miles away.

My last problem was to establish my orientation in the water so that I would know in what direction to look:

It is the twenty second of April, the sun is in the Northern Hemisphere and has just completed four months of northerly travel since it started northward on December twenty first which is mid-winter night, the night following my birthday.

The sun does not travel north and south at a uniform speed, but moves more rapidly near the equator. Having made four out of the six months of northerly travel, it is now one month north of the equator and will continue its northward travel for another two months. Therefore, assume that the sun is now a little more than one third of the way from the equator to the Tropic of Cancer. I cannot remember the latitude of the Tropic of Cancer,[91] but Honolulu Hawaii, my destination, is a little more than twenty degrees North and it is south of the Tropic of Cancer. If I assume that the Tropic of Cancer is somewhat more than 20 degrees north of the equator and that the sun is a little more than one third of the distance between the equator and the Tropic of Cancer, then the sun will rise at about 080 degrees True. That is, one third plus a little, times twenty degrees plus a little, equals about ten degrees plus or minus a couple of degrees. Therefore, the sun should rise at my assumed direction for *Haleakala*.

I then formulated my survival plan:

I will wait until daylight and then look for the rafts in the west (at 260 degrees True) which I can tell because it will be the direction in which my head will cast a shadow on my upraised hand. I will not start swimming until I have actually spotted them in order not to get further away from both the rafts and the boat.

---

[91] 23°27'N, a slip of the memory.

144

I will swim for the first raft I see and get aboard it. If Sadie is aboard, I'll reattach the flare gun to my harness and wait with her on the raft for another airplane. If Sadie and my flare gun are not aboard the first raft I get to, I will stand up on the edge of the raft as high as I can to see if another raft is visible. If I can see another raft where Sadie might be, I'll swim to it. Otherwise, I'll make the first raft I get to, be my home until help arrives.[92]

Easter Sunday

With my plans made I waited for dawn in quiet contemplation. There was nothing more I could do in the dead of night. All my hopes were based on what I could do with the coming of dawn. I now felt totally and absolutely alone. It seemed so long ago when Sadie and I celebrated our last supper south of the equator. Little had I known then that it would be our last supper ever aboard *Haleakala*, and now it appeared that it might possibly have been our last supper forever.

---

[92]Some readers who have not known me before they read this book have expressed doubts that I, or anyone else in the position that I was in, would think like this. Not only are these my thoughts to the best of my recollection but the people who know me best agree that I would think these kind of thoughts in this situation. Although many of my thoughts were surely sub-linguistic, expressing them on paper is difficult without using natural language (English) constructs.

I was tempted to draw diagrams on the paper to explain my thinking during this critical analysis phase. However, I do not think graphically any more than linguistically and I had no drawings at the time. Therefore, the verbal description is the most accurate presentation of what I was thinking.

I was not the only one for whom this was to be a special dawn. Even while I had gone from one disaster to another, people all over the world had been gathering for Easter Sunday sunrise services. Although alone in body, in spirit I would share this dawn with untold millions of other people.

I had reached the point where *the end is probable*.

SAR documentation describes what to expect from the way people handle this, *the ultimate crisis*. Under such monumental stress, normal able-bodied, logical thinking people typically become unable to accomplish even simple tasks or to assist in their own rescue in any way. While some few are calm and rational, most others are hysterical or stunned and bewildered. Those who remain passive usually die quickly unless rescued at once. Deliberate suicide, the furthermost thing from my thoughts at the time, is not at all rare when no way out can be seen.[93]

Even to my own amazement, I still felt in control and determined to use every resource of my mind and body to save myself. If I could be saved, my rescue depended on help from others, but it was up to me to make such rescue possible.

I was anxiously awaiting the first light of the sun to be able to find refuge in the form of a life raft or possibly the overturned boat. Although I was full of hope, I recognized the likelihood I would not see another sunrise. The real possibility,

---

[93]Because the psychological response of a disaster victim is so important to survival, a more complete description and discussion of the stress of the will-to-survive/will-to-die conflict is included in the epilogue starting on page 253.

even great probability, of death before sundown made me say aloud: "This may be my last dawn."

Although not fatalistic, I fully understood the overwhelming probability against survival. But, rather than dwelling on such morbid thoughts, I now had accepted being shipwrecked in its most positive light—as the greatest and most crucial challenge of my life. Having accepted the gauntlet, I then became curious about what "my last dawn" would be like. I had seen spectacular sunrises at sea, and I was hoping for a magnificent spectacle as a sign of encouragement to continue the struggle for survival.

While sailing, the early morning hours before sunrise were always rejuvenating. If I were awake just before sunrise, I would go out on deck and watch for the first signs of La, the Hawaiian name of the sun god. It is easy to see why primitive peoples thought of the sun as a god. I was so impressed by this early morning awe inspiring feeling of the sun as the source of all life in the world that I gave the name *Haleakala* meaning "house of the sun" to the catamaran I designed and built. Now the thought crossed my mind: "How dramatic or maybe ironic! Here I am waiting for La to rise from his home, *Haleakala*, and to thereby point the way to safety."

Elli always said I do things in the most dramatic way. I had to admit her point certainly must be valid. What could be more dramatic and terrifying than my predicament? Surely the Coast Guard had notified her of all of the details. And no one in the world could possibly know that I was still alive, floating in the water, and waiting for dawn. Whatever they had told her must have been the worst possible news. Probably she had been told that I was "Lost at sea and presumed dead."

But I was not dead. I was not sinking into a watery grave. If anything, I felt "reborn" from the depths of disaster. My growing enthusiasm was irrational in light of my dire circumstances, but I had rested and had regained my strength after the exhaustion of the previous day and night. I was convinced I was going to live. I was going to return to life and to Elli!

In barren places such as in the desert or the open sea, one can sense dawn long before there is any apparent light from the sun. There is a feeling that something is about to happen, and I felt the coming of the sun that morning more intensely than ever before. This would be the most crucial morning of my life, and I was determined to see the following sunset. In the dark I could do nothing more; in the light I would have my chance to survive.

My thoughts returned to my plan of action to look for the rafts. I considered I might not be able to see the rafts because they were so low in the water. The boat on the other hand was much higher than the rafts but it was also much further away. If I could see nothing, neither rafts nor boat, it would be better to go for the boat because of the survival supplies I knew to be aboard, even if they were hazardous to retrieve from inside. I knew the rafts had nothing.

The advantage of trying for the rafts instead of the boat was not only that they were much closer, but that they were a bright orange color, designed to be easily spotted from the air, much more so than the dull red of the bottom paint on *Haleakala*. The rafts also had Sadie and I wanted to rescue her if it was at all possible without putting my own life in greater jeopardy, notwithstanding that I was already in about as much jeopardy as possible.

I became aware that the sky was gradually getting lighter. Where moments before there were innumerable stars and the milky way all aglow, the stars now were fading from sight. Slowly I could tell that it was lighter in one direction of the sky than in the other. The clouds on the horizon slowly became visible. The sky became brighter as I stared toward the east. This dawn would be for my eyes only.

Sunrise

I anxiously awaited this Easter sunrise. When it finally came I witnessed one of the <u>least</u> spectacular sunrises I have ever seen! What a disappointment! And I had been so excited, so expectant! I could not even see the sun at first light because it was behind a rain squall. Apparently I was not to get a sign of encouragement in the sky. It was gray and cloudy at the horizon, and the sun continued to be blocked by clouds as it rose. But I had no more time to look at the disappointing sunrise. Now was the time I had been waiting for, and I had to get busy!

I turned around in the water and held my hand up to get the direction of the shadow; no shadow! I turned half way back toward the sun and estimated a half circle around the horizon (to 260 degrees True) and stared and stared in that direction. Nothing! Then I did a full turn very slowly looking at the horizon all the way around. I saw nothing at all the entire way around until I got back to the sun. I did the same thing again. All the way around, very slowly. Again nothing! Then I turned for a third time, even more slowly. Nothing!

I was bobbing alone in the ocean, and the only things I felt sure I had going for me were that the Coast Guard knew I had a genuine emergency, that the plane had found me, and that they knew exactly where I was in the ocean and would be able to find me again.[94] However, was the single rescue effort last night to be the only attempt to help me?

After I had scanned the horizon slowly for the fourth time to no avail, I again considered my alternatives. I had the vague impression I had seen a wink of orange out of the corner of my eye on one of my slow circuits of the horizon. I carefully reconsidered the impression while I continued to stare in that direction until I finally decided what I thought I had seen had been wishful thinking, more of a hallucination than a fact. I wanted desperately to see the orange and perhaps tried to convince myself I had seen something[95] when nothing was there.

_____

[94]My assumptions were quite optimistic. Luckily, I did not know at the time that there is an absolute limit to the distance the Coast Guard will go to attempt a Mayday rescue, and I was at the limit!

[95]I may have actually seen one of the rafts, but at the time I did not trust my own sighting, and it is very doubtful that the rafts could have been seen under the most propitious circumstances.

150

I did not yet want to start out swimming unless I saw something! Inaction would surely be deadly too, and I would soon have to chose a direction in which to swim even without having seen anything. But first I still desperately wanted to have some indication before starting out.

To increase my chances of survival, which I now realized was nearly impossible, I had to get to either the raft or the boat. I had chosen to go for the rafts at first light assuming that I would be able to see them at dawn. Now I realized that I would have little chance of seeing either the boat or the rafts. I had decided that if neither was visible, the boat was a better destination. I now chose to swim for the boat. It was much larger and therefore a better target to be seen from the air. Most importantly, it had the supplies I needed, particularly fresh water. And finally, from my position on the surface of the water I might be able to see the larger boat further away and also be seen further away on it than on the smaller raft. Even though it was probably too far away for me to reach, it was the best choice I had.

The sun had come out and was now clearly visible between the clouds. It was time to go.[96] I picked out the spot below and now a little to the left of the moving sun where I

---

[96] It was about twenty minutes after six in the morning when I began swimming for the wreckage. Even without a watch I could be very sure of the time. Every day of the year the sun rises at exactly six am local apparent time. At the center of a time zone in mid ocean, the zone time is the same as the local apparent time. I was nearly at the center of a time zone at the equator so I knew that the sun rose at exactly six am.

thought the boat had to be and started staring at the target while swimming toward that point.

As I swam, I continued to stare at that one point. For nearly a half hour I swam without seeing anything. Then I decided if I did not see anything in that direction for another half hour I would consider going the opposite way toward where I though the rafts to be. I did not see any other alternative, even though if I had to go back, I would wasted two hours of hard swimming just to get back to where I started. I was just about ready to stop swimming east when I saw a flash!

Rescue Operations

During the early morning hours, while I was deciding where to swim, the JRCC was busy planning the rescue operations.

By dawn the scheduled mission for CG-1414 had changed because of the mechanical problems which made the planned early arrival on station impossible. Priority now was given to relocation of the rafts and survivor. At 9:30, instead of departing for Christmas Island, CG-1414 was now to fly directly to 00°34.1'N 164°43.7'W, the location of the rafts MAC-38084 had dropped. After an initial search CG-1414 was to fly back to Christmas Island for refueling. The latest plan still called for CG-1414 to return to the scene after refueling to either fly one more relocate mission if the first was unsuccessful, or to provide cover over the drifting survivor. In either case, they were to remain on scene the second time until relieved by AFR-823 from Hickam Air Force Base. After relief CG-1414 was to return to Christmas Island for the night.

The Air Force C-130, Flight AFR-823, was scheduled to depart Honolulu at 3:30 p.m., arrive on station by night fall, 6:30 p.m., and relieve CG-1414. AFR-823 would provide cover or continue the search, if necessary to relocate the rafts, and vector the *Discoverer* to the scene to pick up the survivor. The estimated time of arrival of the *Discoverer* was still 11 p.m. that night.

The status of the rescue operation at that point was summarized in a status report wire[97] to all of the Air Force bases and command centers which might be involved in the SAR mission.

Mechanical repair of CG-1414 continued for two more hours, and it became apparent the plane would not be ready for its scheduled departure. Moreover, missing the scheduled departure would interrupt the remaining time table. Yet another new time table was needed contingent on the completion of repairs.

22 APR 2036Z (1036W) Barbers Point, 10:36 a.m.

Repairs were finally complete and CG-1414, now with Lieutenant Junior Grade Farrow commanding, again departed

---

[97]The flare that MAC-38084 reported dropping at 22 April 1250Z was not seen by me. The flare I launched was fired to attract the attention of the plane that I only saw by its searching lights (probably the landing lights).

Document 13.
22 APR 1800Z (0800W) 8:00 a.m. Telex (page 1 of 3).

FROM JRCC
TO <Nineteen Air Force Bases and command centers.>

1. RESCUE OPENING REPORT: 22 APR 1005Z.

2. MISSION NUMBER: PAC-014A-22 APR.

3. SITUATION: SAILING VESSEL HALEAKALA TAKING ON
WATER.

    A.   DESCRIPTION OF SAR OBJECTIVE:

    (1)   56 FOOT TWIN HULLED CATAMARAN (US)
(REGISTRATION NUMBER 597789) WITH WHITE
PONTOONS PAINTED DARK RED BELOW WATER LINE.

    (2)   TYPE OF FLIGHT/FLOAT PLAN AND ROUTE OF
FLIGHT/FLOAT PLAN:
        DEPARTURE POINT UNKNOWN.
        DESTINATION HONOLULU, HAWAII.

    (3)   PILOT'S OR CAPTAIN'S NAME AND ADDRESS:
        NOT RELEASABLE AT THIS TIME.

    (4)   NUMBER OF PEOPLE ON BOARD: ONE.

    (5)   SIGNIFICANT WEATHER ALONG FLIGHT/FLOAT
PLAN:
        SEAS 4-7 FEET, WINDS EAST NORTHEAST 8 TO 15
KNOTS WITH GUSTS OF 20 TO 30 KNOTS. CLOUD
COVER 2000 FEET BROKEN TO SCATTERED.
SCATTERED THUNDERSHOWERS.

Barbers Point in route to 00°34.1'N 164°43.7'W. Droppable

Document 14.

22 APR 1800Z (0800W) 8:00 a.m. Telex (page 2 of 3).

---

(6) KNOWN SURVIVAL EQUIPMENT ON BOARD: LIFE JACKETS, FLARES. SIGNALING DEVICES, EPIRB/ELT ON 121.5 MHZ. VESSEL HAS DINGY BUT NO LIFE RAFT. OPERATOR IS WELL EXPERIENCED SAILOR TRAINED IN SURVIVAL TECHNIQUES.

(7) LAST KNOWN POSITION:
00-50-04N 164-35-04W, APPROXIMATELY 360 NAUTICAL MILES WEST OF CHRISTMAS ISLAND.

B. ACTIONS TAKEN:
(1) CONTROLLING AGENCY: JRCC HONOLULU, HI.
(2) 22 APR 0310Z SAR FORCES ALERTED.
(3) 22 APR 1005Z SAR FORCES LAUNCHED.

C. PERSONNEL INFORMATION:
ONE PERSON INVOLVED, ONE PERSON MISSING.

D. FLYING ACTIVITY:

UNIT	SORTIES	FLYING HOURS
CG-1414	01	1.0

E. NUMBER OF PERSONS SAVED: NONE.

F. FUTURE PLANS:

(1) ELT/EPIRB AND FLARE SEARCH BEGINNING AT LAST KNOWN POSITION.

(2) SAR FORCES AVAILABLE FOR SEARCH:
HC-130P FROM 6594TESTG,
HC-130 FROM USCG DISTRICT 14
NOAA RESEARCH VESSEL DISCOVERER.

---

radios, datum marker buoys, food, water, and rafts were aboard.

Document 15.

22 APR 1800Z (0800W) 8:00 a.m. Telex (page 3 of 3).

G. NARRATIVE SUMMARY OF SAR ACTIONS:

(1) 22 APR 0330Z LAST COMMUNICATION WITH
SUBJECT VESSEL.
(2) 22 APR 0400Z VESSEL MISSED HIS
COMMUNICATION SCHEDULE.
(3) 22 APR 1005Z MAC-38084 DEPARTED Pago Pago.
(4) 22 APR 1242Z CG-1414 DEPARTED FOR
CHRISTMAS ISLAND.
(5) 22 APR 1340Z CG-1414 RETURNED DUE TO
MECHANICAL TROUBLE.
(6) 22 APR 1250Z MAC-38084 ARRIVED ON SCENE.
AIRCRAFT DROPPED A FLARE AND DISTRESSED
VESSEL FIRED ONE FLARE BACK. POSITION IS
00-34.1N 164-43.7W. THREE LIFE RAFTS WERE
DEPLOYED BY MAC-38084. ELT/EPIRB IS BEING HEARD
ON 121.5 MHZ AND 242.0 MHZ WHICH IS COMING
FROM PARTIALLY SUBMERGED VESSEL.
(7) 22 APR 1645Z AIRCRAFT COULD NOT LOCATE
PERSON ON BOARD AFTER SUNRISE.
(8) 22 APR 1655Z MAC-38084 DEPARTED FOR HICKAM
AIR FORCE BASE.
(9) 22 APR 2100Z MAC-38084 ESTIMATED TIME OF
ARRIVAL IN HAWAII.

But because of the additional hour delay in departure there would be no time for a second search mission before dark. Now, after only one brief initial search, the plane must fly on to Christmas Island for the night.

This raised considerable doubt about achieving the SAR objective for a minimum of seventy-eight percent probability of detection of wreckage and/or survivor, as defined in the Search

Plan.[98] A single abbreviated search of part of area B-2 would be all that CG-1414 could accomplish before being forced to depart the scene due to low fuel reserves. This greatly reduced the already slim chance of success.

Flash Of Light

While swimming in the direction in which I hoped to find the boat, I had seen a flash of light. It was in nearly the same direction[99] that I assumed I would find it, although a little further south than I had calculated the boat to be.

I did not stop swimming while I considered whether the flash could be something other than the boat. I was quite convinced whatever I had seen was man-made and not a jumping fish or water reflection, and I immediately increased my pace, swimming harder in the direction of the flash.

As I swam, I thought about the conditions which could affect such a flash of sunlight. I realized I had seen the flash as

---

[98]See the telex on page 111.

[99]I had expected to see the boat to the left of the rising sun while the flash appeared just to the right of the sun, at about 085 to 090 degrees True, according to my mental arithmetic. It was impossible to tell what I had seen, but it was definitely something other than just the sparkle of the ocean. Such a blink of light could have been a reflection from one of the rafts but only if I was completely wrong in my analysis of their relative direction.

I was rising up on a swell. Since I rose up on a passing swell every ten minutes or so, surely I should have seen more flashes. I knew I had not seen a flash on each rise of the sea even though my field of vision was increased by about the same distance each time. However, a small squall had been forming between me and the flash and it might have hidden an intermediate flash. Whatever the source of the flash, I figured I probably could only see it when the flashing object too was rising on a swell.

It occurred to me the flash might be a reflection from the bridge of a rescue ship. If so, then swimming for it would not be of any particular value, but it certainly wouldn't hurt my chances of rescue. If it were not a rescue vessel, then I had to come to some conclusion pretty soon to support my decision about swimming on or turning back.

I could think of nothing on the rafts that would flash in the sunlight while there were several possible sources on the boat. The ports of the capsized *Haleakala* were below the surface and could not flash unless the trim had changed to such an extent that one side was much higher and out of the water. This was not very probable. So I concluded that the rudders would be the most likely source of the flash. They were large and relatively flat and the most reflective surface still above the water. They were also the highest points having been designed to extend six inches below the keel.[100]

If the reflection had come from the rudders they would not line up correctly for a flash every time I bobbed up. From

---

[100]This extension was constructed as a break-away section to spare the rudder post in case of grounding.

my education as a physicist[101] I knew the sun would have to be reflecting along a grazing angle across the rudders so the dull finish of the paint would be balanced by the low angle of incidence making a good reflection.

I worked through this analysis as I continued swimming, although I did not see anything else for yet another half hour. I swam on, partly on conviction, partly on faith that I was going in the right direction. Then a second flash in exactly the same place! I was thrilled! I was certain the two flashes I had seen had to be from the boat.

I started swimming even harder. It was as fast as I thought I could possibly go and still be able to swim all day if necessary. If I swam too slowly, the boat would move further and further away from me. If I swam too fast, I would not be able to keep up the pace, and I might well lose the boat and my life when I became exhausted. I had to forcibly overcome the natural tendency to swim as hard as I could and instead set a hard but steady pace.

For over twenty minutes I swam with my eyes glued to the target direction.

As I swam, waves splashed in my face and drove water down my nose. I tried to avoid choking on the water by protecting my nose from the waves. Whenever I saw a larger

---

[101]My first professional career was as a physicist, followed by several others, and one might say that the last one apparently was going to be marine architect and boat builder. Before embarking on the job of designing and building *Haleakala*, I read that no amateur can build a boat over 40 feet long. I found that this advice was correct but in a backward way: "If you build a boat over 40 feet long, you ain't no amateur."

wave coming I raised my hands in front of my face the way I had done the night before.

Again I saw another flash! I now started to time the flashes with my watch.

Little jellyfish stung me as I swam. They were only about an inch in diameter and their sting more annoying than painful. Figuring they would not be a real hazard to me, I tried to ignore them but I did swim around any I saw in my path.

The next flash was in twenty minutes followed by one in eighteen. The two were closer together!

I swam for hour upon hour encouraged by more and more frequent sightings. I knew then I would make it aboard. I could not and would not stop swimming!

At last, I reached a point were I could see the flashes were definitely coming from the boat. I was excited and unconsciously started swimming faster than the pace I had set for myself.

With the increased effort I started to get out of breath. When I was sure I was gaining on my refuge I stopped for a short rest. Immediately my legs started to cramp! I quickly resumed swimming again but at a slower rate and paying more attention to pacing myself.

At first only a glimpse of the boat would appear, so little and so quickly that I would not have been sure what it was if I didn't know that there was no other possibility. Then one time the boat rose high enough for me to clearly see the top of both rudders above the waves. Then I could see progressively a little more of the boat clearly each time as it rose above the horizon, and it stayed visible longer before again sinking out of sight. Slowly it seemed that we were again both in the same sea,

Haleakala and I. At the top of one large wave it seemed as if I had climbed a hill and could look down on my destination.

At last it was in sight continuously.

The distance could now be judged and it was clear the distance was shrinking.

I was now in her presence[102]—she lay about a hundred yards off.

As I covered the last yards, I considered where it would be easiest to get back aboard. While still twenty yards away, she slowly turned to present her port aft quarter. I had to change course and swim around to the right and up to the trailing edge of the wing.

All of a sudden I was aboard!

I had been swimming all morning, from shortly after dawn through noon and into the afternoon. I had attained my goal. I was back aboard the *Haleakala* raft!

Both elated and exhausted[103] I felt the way I think runners feel when they finish a marathon.[104] I climbed up onto

---

[102]This feeling of being together was partly due to the fact that, until I swam for the rafts, I had never been further away from any vessel at sea. Now I was again at the maximum safe range. This is the distance that we would swim out around the boat during mid ocean swimming parties.

[103]My long swim had totally exhausted me, and I would remain sore for many days.

[104]I had successfully completed my own marathon, a marathon swim I thought could have been as much as several miles! The boat could have been as much as three miles away when I started swimming and it could have gone another two or three miles as I swam to catch up. Could I have covered that

(continued...)

the keel, lay down on top of it, closed my eyes and immediately was asleep. But I did not sleep long.

My habit of taking short naps made me ready to go again in a short time. In spite of my deep fatigue, I awoke in less than an hour. I felt recovered from the immediate effects of my long swim and a lot more refreshed than I had been when I climbed out of the sea. I could not consider a longer rest because I had so much more to do, and the adrenaline masked my weariness.

My first priority was retrieving the emergency water from under the dinghy beneath the stern of the capsized *Haleakala*. (I could last no more than a week without water in the 90° heat.)

Last night (was it only last night?) the acid, oil, and darkness had made diving for the water impossible. Now I would be able to dive down again and reclaim it.

---

[104](...continued)

distance? I was too tired to think any more about it at that time.

I had stopped paying attention to the time after the first couple of hours of swimming and did not note the time of arrival back at the boat. It may have also been that the sails came loose and went deeper in the water creating more drag and slowing the forward porposing motion. These suggestions are made because even considering how dedicated I was to survival, and the physical condition I was in, such a long swim in this time seems improbable in retrospect. In any case, whatever the distance and time, for me it was a marathon.

Search for Water

I jumped down from the keel and went back to the stern to begin my search for water. I took off my life jacket and securely fastened it to the prop shaft. I would not be able to dive under the boat while wearing the life jacket on but I kept wearing the harness, knife, whistle, and light.

Before entering the water, I looked carefully to make sure there were no sharks around the boat. Concern for sharks was once again a reasonable precaution since I now could protect myself by not entering shark infested waters. I no longer ignored the danger from sharks as I had the night before.

Slipping over the side, I swam down under the aft deck to retrieve one of the water bottles. Acid and oil still flowed back from the engine compartment. But although it still stung my eyes, it was no longer unbearable. I saw the dinghy had been swept away, but the water bottles were still securely lashed down as I had left them. I cut one bottle free and brought it up to the surface. When I set it up on the wing bottom I noticed the side of the bottle was broken. I removed the cap to taste the water. It was salty!

Immediately I went back into the water, dove down, and retrieved the remaining bottle. As I brought it up I saw the cap was gone. I tasted the water to make sure; it too was salt water. There seemed no difference in the taste of the water in my two bottles and the taste of the ocean. I now realized I was going to be without the fresh water that had been the primary target of my long swim.

I deliberately threw the two bottles overboard and watched them float off to remove the temptation to drink from them later. In retrospect, I should not have abandoned the water bottles. Although they were quite brackish, they might still have been less salty than the pure seawater. If I did get to the point where I would consider drinking salt water, it would have been better to drink this mixture than drink directly from the ocean. But, at the time I thought it safer to remove the temptation.

I then began a series of short inspection dives under the boat. Starting at the bow I dove down along the edge of the hull. I wanted to see what the conditions were below and what I might find that I could use for survival. I was quite happy to see the forward hatches were still dogged down, and the contents of those bow compartments should still be intact though probably flooded. The main fresh water tanks were in these compartments, and I had every reason to believe they would be intact.

Underwater I found a piece of light line tangled in a piece of carpet approximately two feet by two feet square. I brought both up and put them safely on the keel. On my next dive I saw a large piece of the companionway steps caught under the boat and retrieved it.

As I continued my underwater inspection, I noticed the 65 pound plow anchor had broken through the hatch of the starboard forward stateroom and hung straight down on 600 feet of 3/4 inch anchor rode with the bitter end still belayed. If it appeared useful to me later, I might be able to get a hold of the line and pull it up. I completed my inspection tour and climbed out of the water to rest and to think about my situation.

I was now so tired I feared my judgment might well be getting faulty. Becoming overly tired while on a solo crossing was a very real danger, and I always tried to make a conscious effort to keep from getting exhausted to the point where my judgment could be dangerously flawed. Therefore, I climbed back aboard, put my life jacket back on and crawled up on top of the keel trying to stay as much out of the sun as I could manage.

It was time for a time of rest and reanalysis. I searched my pockets to see if I had anything else with me. I still had five flare cartridges in my pockets but no launcher, since I had left my flare gun on the raft with Sadie. I found a pair of pliers I had somehow left in my pocket when I heard the big bang and had forgotten until now. Perhaps I could use the flares with the pliers. I had one flashlight battery that I put back in my pocket, although I should have thrown it away since it was probably dead, in any case useless, and the acid could have made a nasty burn through the material of the pocket.

In addition to harness and life jacket, I was still wearing the thin, ripped T-shirt and cutoff jeans which left my legs, arms, and head exposed, affording little protection from the elements. Although like most sailors, I had a reasonably good tan, I had also had a lot of exposure already and was beginning to burn from the prolonged exposure in the bright sun. It was afternoon and I normally stayed out of the noon day sun.

To protect myself as well as I could I made use of the few things I had found. I positioned the companionway step on top of the keel to fashion a small sun shade. Covering my legs as much as possible with the piece of carpet to shield them from the direct sun, I put my head and shoulders under the step, and folded my arms over my chest in order to also keep my upper arms in the shade.[105]

In the shade of my improvised shelter I rested and worked on my number one problem: Water! I had been without water for a day and a half and could certainly use a drink. But, although I was thirsty, I was not yet to the point where water had become a maddening preoccupation.[106]

Lack of food was much less of a problem. I certainly could live without food for quite some time as long as I had water. But if I could not get water, food would become the pressing problem. I knew I would get some water from the digestion of food, and the cases of canned food aboard included fruits and vegetables packed with a lot of water.

---

[105]Until now I had not realized personal survival gear should include protection from sunburn. When sailing in heavy weather in colder climates, I nearly always wore my float coat for safety and for protection from the cold. But a coat can also provide important protection from the sun as well as from the cold. So now, in addition to wearing my float coat in heavy weather in cold climates, I also keep it handy in nice warm weather even in tropical climates. Although I would have preferred a hat with a visor, the protection provided by the drawstring hood would have been quite welcome in the broiling sun as I lay on the keel. Later that night the warmth of the jacket would have been most comforting.

[106]My thirst may have been greater than usual because I habitually drink quite a lot of water, six to eight quarts a day in the hot sticky heat of the tropics.

In hot weather adequate water is important, and many newcomers to the tropics or desert have to learn to force feed themselves with water.

There was plenty of water in the four main bow water tanks plus the one auxiliary tank inside the boat. The auxiliary tank was mounted in the galley overhead[107] as a gravity feed tank for daily fresh water usage. It was vented and probably was now contaminated with salt water through the open vent. The other tanks were also vented but I had shut off these vents (one of the items on the check list) before I set sail, and I only opened them while underway when actually transferring water from the main tanks to the auxiliary tank.

The main tanks consisted of four 30-gallon tanks, two in each bow. And, most importantly, these bow tanks were directly accessible through deck hatches, now underwater beneath each bow. Even if one or more of the four tanks had been damaged, at least one should have remained intact, and one tank would have enough fresh water to sustain me for weeks! Even assuming the compartments were flooded, I worked out how I could rig up one of the vent hoses to suck fresh water from the tanks while I held my breath on a quick dive under the bow.

Should the water tanks be contaminated or destroyed, then there remained great stores of food aboard, but they would be much harder to access than the water in the tanks. The food was accessible only by entering the main salon under water, a quite hazardous undertaking. Overturned, the main cabin was relatively deep in the water. I would have to dive down about six feet to get under the cabin top, then swim across another ten feet under the boat to enter through one of the "overhead" hatches. I would then quickly have to find whatever I was after, in darkness and amid a considerable amount of flotsam. And

---

[107]For non-sailors, the galley overhead is the kitchen ceiling.

after finding what I needed, I would then have to return the way I had entered all the while holding my breath. How long would all this take, and how long could I hold my breath?

Another possibility was to dive down and enter the boat as before, but then to swim across the cabin and come up inside one of the air pockets that must be in each hull. This would have to be done in almost total darkness because I expected there was little light in the hulls. The advantage would be that I then could go back and forth between the air pocket and the rest of the boat while I searched inside. Swimming inside the hull would be easier than the outside diving approach which was made doubly difficult by the half knot current caused by the forward motion of the boat.

If I decided to enter the cabin from below, it would be a formidable task, and at the moment the hazard of the attempt outweighed the need of getting anything useful out of the central part of the boat. I decided I would not attempt it until I has a much greater need for supplies. I would certainly wait until morning before taking the risk of the dive. However, I planned to make a very strong attempt the next day. While I had not yet decided on a do-or-die attempt, I felt I could not wait too long and risk becoming too weak to be able to accomplish the task.

While these thoughts ran through my mind I was lying on the keel under my improvised little sun shade ten yards ahead of the rudder. I was too far forward to run a safety line around the prop shaft and clip it back on my harness as I had the night before, and I considered running a separate line back from my perch to tie myself off. The line I had found was quite long enough, but I concluded it was not necessary. In the good weather, with only about five foot seas, if I were to fall off the keel while asleep, I would wake up and simply climb back. While lying on top of the keel with these thoughts my eyes closed, and I fell asleep for a second time.

I awoke about an hour later and scanned the horizon for any signs of rescue. When I was satisfied nothing was in sight, I checked for sharks in the water below then jumped down into the water to cool off and wet my clothing. I dunked my head and held it under for a moment being careful not to drink any seawater. Cooled off and somewhat refreshed, I climbed back up on the boat and went back to the piece of boarding ladder still lashed to the prop shaft at the stern.

Climbing up the ladder I again scanned the horizon for any ships or planes.[108] I also thought about cutting through the wing bottom to get at the supplies. But the double decking of the wing bottom, a total of one inch of wood, would be quite difficult with only my rigging knife, but I would consider it again if I was unable to get supplies by diving. I had ruled out going through the hull to get water. It would be easier to reach the water tanks just inside the bow hatches by diving than by cutting a hole in the hull.

---

[108]I realized later that although I am nearsighted and did not have my contact lenses, I had been seeing quite clearly for long distances without them. This was probably partly due to the "pin hole" effect caused by the bright sunshine. And some of my visual acuity might also have been due to my strong desire to see things on the horizon.

Second SAR Search

While I had been on the marathon swim back to the boat it had been a busy day for many others in Honolulu.[109] After hours of repair, CG-1414 had finally become airborne over Hawaii. The flight was now eight and a half hours late, a full three and a half hours after the initially planned landing in Christmas Island for refueling. With no time remaining to be able to stage from Christmas, CG-1414 was proceeding directly to the Mayday site, still more than four and a half hours away.

23 APR 0145Z (1445X) CG-1414, 00°34'N 164°43'W (estimate), 2:45 p.m.

A little over five hours after leaving Honolulu, CG-1414 reported they had entered the search area to begin the second search for rafts and survivor. Apparently they still had instrument problems because instead of giving a fix, they gave only an estimate of their position as 00-34'N 164-43'W at 3:50 p.m. in Honolulu (0150Z). CG-1414 then proceeded down the vessel dead reckoned drift (245 True) for 25 nautical miles. It

---

[109]Going back in time for the reader.

was another twenty five minutes[110] before CG-1414 reported beginning the actual search pattern.

23 APR 0220Z (1520X) CG-1414, Search area, 3:20 p.m.

At twenty minutes after three, CG-1414 commenced an expanding square search pattern down wind from the position of the flare sighting and raft drop by MAC-38084 the previous night. Search conditions were reported to be excellent. The wind was coming from the east northeast at 10 knots. The seas were four feet and the visibility was 15 to 20 miles.

In spite of the reported lack of detection of an EPIRB[111] by the Air Pacific Flight 551 overflight the evening before, CG-1414 now reported loud and clear reception of the EPIRB SOS beacon on 121.5 Mhz. However, the UHF direction finding equipment on board was inoperative, and they were not certain of the direction to the boat.[112] Moreover, it was the rafts, not the boat they were attempting to find, assuming that I

---

[110]A C-130 flies at about 280 knots and it could have arrived at the beginning of the search pattern in five or six minutes. However, the plane probably reduced speed to a search rather than cruising speed as it entered the general search area and most likely was already searching for the last twenty minutes before reporting arrival at the target destination.

[111]Note that of all the reports of hearing the EPIRB, only Flight 551 failed to detect its emissions when they were within range and listening.

[112]The electronic location transmitters dropped by MAC-38084 had already been reported as inoperative by the flight that dropped them. The EPIRB on the wreckage would then have been the best hope for electronic location. The lack of operational UHF direction finding equipment on board the Coast Guard SAR flight then becomes doubly surprising even though it would not necessarily have helped on the mission to locate the rafts. See page 136.

was most probably back on a raft. But the worst news yet; they estimated they would not be able to remain searching on the scene for more than another 25 minutes.

23 APR 0200Z (1600W) CG-1414, End search, 4:00 p.m.

Although the search plane did not report the time that the expanding square search pattern was abandoned, time-and-distance calculations indicate that the search was abandoned at this time.

22 APR 0230Z (1630W) Honolulu, 4:30 p.m.

JRCC called and briefed Elli as soon as they got the latest bad news. While they were talking to her, CG-1414 began to report the results of their search.

Coast Guard Plane

Atop the keel I was again scanning the horizon for what seemed the millionth time that afternoon. My eyes kept searching the horizon for ships or planes almost constantly, although I had no idea of how long I would have to wait—hours, days, weeks?.

While watching for planes in all directions, I began to plan my evening actions. I would again use my broken ladder and wedge between the rudder and prop. The life jacket would again be my cushion against the sharp blades of the prop. There was not much chance of getting much sleep but I wanted to search in the dark for planes anyway. I hoped, but doubted, I could set off a flare. The main thing I could do is make sure that my strobes were clearly visible from as high a point as possible. If I heard or saw anything, I would again stand up on the keel to make as large a target as possible.

In the quiet[113] afternoon, I began to hear the distant mummer of thunder or the faint sound of an engine. The sound slowly rose in intensity until it was clearly the sound of an airplane engine. Staring in the direction of the sound I saw an airplane far away, slowly coming into view, a little north of the western horizon. I must have shouted for joy!

Just hearing the sound of a plane meant that they were looking for me. Otherwise, they would be much too high to be heard. This one was low enough to be searching and therefore must be trying to find me.

I was thrilled that they were there but worried that they might not see me. Many stories are told by survivors of having spotted ships and been unable to get their attention even with

---

[113]It is not unusual for it to be very quiet at sea. It is normally much more quiet at sea than at most places ashore. Rachel Carson's title *Silent Spring* emphasizes the background noise of insects and birds on land, both missing deep at sea. There are none of the common sounds of the machinery of civilization when the ship's engine has been stopped. Under sail there is the sound of the wind through the rigging but it is more quiet than the breeze through the trees. The very few planes are at such high altitude that they cannot be heard. Other ships, even when approaching near enough to recognize people aboard, do not make enough sound to be heard. The waves do lap on the hulls making about as much noise as a babbling brook, that is when the weather is not howling.

flares across the bow.[114] One told of firing a bullet into the bridge of a passing freighter which finally got their attention after repeated flares had been unsuccessful.

I was further encouraged by seeing the plane in the direction I expected to find it. I realized I had been spending more of my time looking in that general direction than in any other single direction. I imagine in my subconscious, I thought the most probable direction help would come from was the same direction from which I had come when I swam back to the boat. If I had stayed with the rafts I would be in that direction. In fact, the reason I was now east of the expected position was because the *Haleakala* raft was still "sailing" east.

My immediate reaction was to leap up and down waving my arms and shouting to attract the attention of the airplane. I would have fired a flare but I no longer had my flare gun and had not figured how to use the tool I had to fire it. I decided the most effective thing would be to make the largest possible visible target.

I jumped down, ran back and un-clipped the large strobe light from the prop shaft and then climbed back up on the keel. I held my arms straight out at my sides with the large flashing strobe light in one hand and the smaller one in the other. I stood on top of the keel in the spread-eagle international sign of distress although I realized my additional stature above the fifty foot long keel was most likely insignificant from the air.

---

[114]Modern vessels, including *Haleakala*, frequently sail with no one at the helm, and sometimes with no one on the bridge. It is even rumored that some airplanes on long transoceanic flights fly part of the time with no one in the cockpit.

However, I was doing all I could think of doing to attract attention.

After several minutes the plane <u>turned</u> and started heading my way. Tears of joy welled up as it grew larger, descended to about 300 feet, and flew directly over my head! I maintained my stance although I was sure anyone flying over would know that I was in distress without any "international sign."

I desperately wanted to communicate and considered how to convey a message to the search aircraft using only body language. By standing in this pose I tried to say:

"I am in good enough physical condition to climb up on the keel and stand in this position."

"I am in sufficiently stable mental condition to think of displaying the international distress sign."

"I am calm and am going to help in my rescue in any way I possibly can."[115]

---

[115] As with the Mayday transmission, I now realize this, too, was an unusually cool and calm act, atypical under the circumstances, and hence easily misunderstood. In an absolutely critical life and death situation, insane panic is more common <u>and more easily understood</u> by others. As a matter of fact, potential survivors of shipwreck tragedies have insanely and tragically avoided rescuers! Some form of paranoia caused them to hide when rescue was at hand.

I felt at the time the meaning I intended would be apparent. Subsequently I have been told by experienced search and rescue people that my message was certainly not "misunderstood," instead, it was probably just not "understood" at all!

The plane was clearly marked with a large diagonal red stripe and clear black lettering "COAST GUARD." I recognized it as a

Figure 13 **Coast Guard SAR Plane**

modern "flying boxcar" type airplane (this a C-130) capable of dropping supplies and parachutists.

I immediately jumped back down onto the wing bottom as the plane passed overhead, and I could see the large rear cargo bay door was open. I watched as the plane banked in a tight circle. I fully expected that the crew was going to drop me something. This time I was certainly not going to swim further from the boat than I could easily swim back. I had clearly learned my lesson. Nothing would be worth deserting the *Haleakala* raft. But I wanted to be off the narrow keel, on the wing bottom, and prepared for anything. If they dropped me another raft, I would ignore it. However, if they dropped something else close enough for me to retrieve, I planned to swim for it. I crossed the wing bottom and went back to the stern to be ready to enter the water.

On the next pass they made a drop at a very low altitude. I could see the orange and white parachute and a bright orange cylinder, which turned out to be a five-gallon size metal drum. At the first sight of the orange object, it took all of my attention.

176

I could see it clearly. I quickly estimated it would hit the water ahead and to the right of the boat.

I jumped into the water, still wearing the life jacket, and swam out a few feet to the right of the boat while keeping close track of the drum. As I watched, I realized the parachute trailing out behind the drum acted as a drogue. My initial estimate of the drift of the drum was correct: it was going to pass on the right of the boat. But the major part of the parachute and rigging was going to drift right between the hulls. I would be able to snag the chute and pull up the drum without having to swim for it.

I quickly climbed back aboard the boat, ran up to the bow and went out on the net. The parachute got there almost the instant I did. I grabbed it. The plane had been so accurate in the drop that the parachute would have snagged on the bow if I had not picked it up instead. I was convinced that they could have dropped it into my outstretched arms as I stood on the pitching deck if the circumstances had required it.

I pulled in on the shrouds until I got to the can. As soon as I could reach it, I snapped my safety line onto a D-ring on the side of the can. Now the drum and I would be inseparable! Picking it up together with the parachute, I went back to my station at the stern and clipped myself and the can to the prop shaft. Now the drum and I and the boat were all fastened together as one inseparable unit. I was not going to lose whatever they had dropped me!

I positioned the drum on the top rung of the ladder, draped the parachute over the prop, and tied the drum into position with an extra piece of line. I wanted everything to be secure before I opened it so I could not possibly lose any of the contents. The waves had risen to over six feet since dawn, creating an occasional foot of surf that rushed across the wing bottom and threatened to knock me off of my feet. With the drum secure, I was now prepared to open it.

Easter Basket

The water-tight lid of the drum was held down on a rubber gasket by a sealing ring around the top of the can. The ring was closed by a clamping lever held in place by a small tab, and the tab was fastened by a wire looped through a small eye, its ends twisted together. I untwisted the wire and attempted to pry open the latch securing the lid. It was difficult to open with my fingers but easy to pry up with the marlin spike on my knife. As I opened the drum I carefully held onto the ring and the lid so nothing would get away. I was not too surprised when I looked inside the drum and found jellybeans on top. After all it was Easter Sunday, and jellybeans seemed appropriate[116] in this, my Easter basket from the Coast Guard.

---

[116]Later I found out jelly beans are a Coast Guard "signature" and are put in all survival packages like this, not only the ones dropped on Easter. And they have a very clever reason for putting them in the package. The survivor will surely eat some immediately, as I did, which will calm him down and raise his spirits, and the digested sugar will provide immediate energy and some water. In general, jelly beans can increase anyone's survival potential.

I wonder if President Reagan, who kept a bowl full on his desk, ever thought of this use of jellybeans?

The contents of the drum were packed inside a heavy plastic bag, which was folded down to keep them protected. On top of the plastic bag, in addition to the jellybeans, was a small greenish item wrapped in a sheet of paper. A radio! I popped some more jellybeans in my mouth and picked up the radio. The now clearly olive colored drab radio had white lettering and a black nylon strap and was a little larger and heavier than a compact cassette recorder. I immediately used a piece of my line to attach the radio to my harness. It too was now secure and would not get away even if I should accidentally drop it.

The sheet of paper was held on with a rubber band. Even before I unwrapped it, I knew this must be a two-way radio. It never occurred to me that it could be anything else, although they could well have dropped me an EPIRB with no two-way capability. As I took the paper off I was naturally excited because I knew I would soon be able to reestablish radio contact with my rescuers.

Document 16. Radio Wrapper Message.

THIS RADIO IS ON
PUSH BUTTON ON SIDE
TO TALK.
RELEASE TO LISTEN.

The wrapper was hand printed on a piece of green lined paper as shown. Following the instructions, I pushed the button and said: "Hello airplane. This is the *Haleakala*.[117] Over."

I waited briefly for their response and was surprised at not receiving any acknowledgment. There was a lot of static noise but no answer to my call. I repeated my message: "Hello airplane. This is the *Haleakala*. Over."

Again, no response. With some apprehension I repeated my message for a third time.

I kept my eyes on the plane circling overhead. As it went by I could see a couple of men still standing in the open cargo door. They waved at me as they went by, but I did not read any particular significance in their gestures.[118] The radio still gave me nothing but static.

I decided to examine the radio in more detail to see if I could figure out what was wrong. On the back was a two by two inch panel as illustrated with operating instructions printed with silver letters on a black background.

The function indicator on the front of the radio had an arrow with four alternatives as shown in Figure 15. The arrow was pointing to "VOICE/MCW 243.0." I knew 243.0 MHz was

---

[117]That is exactly what I said, although I don't know why I was so formal. It may have been because I was trying so desperately to survive and I thought that precise communication could be key to survival.

[118]Since I had made gestures that they did not understand, it is entirely possible that they also made gestures that I did not understand.

also the emergency mayday frequency of my EPIRB (in addition to 121.5 MHz). I also knew I had activated it before *Haleakala* capsized. The EPIRB now had been underwater for over twenty-four hours, and I did not expect that it could still be broadcasting with

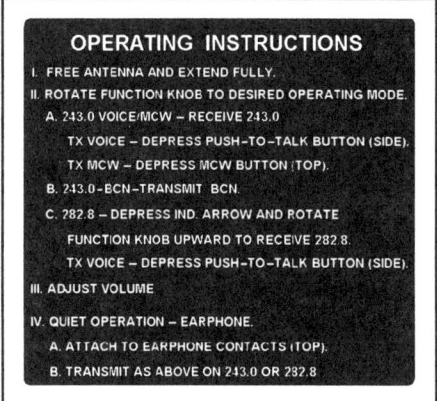

Figure 14 **Radio Back Panel**

the antenna completely submerged. However, since it had an insulated antenna, the noise I heard could be the radio beacon being transmitted by the EPIRB beneath my feet. I looked at the operating instructions again remembering they indicated the radio could also broadcast and receive on another frequency.

I tried to turn the control knob on the side of the radio to move the arrow up from "VOICE/MCW 243.0" past "OFF" to "VOICE 282.8." But I could not move it up past the "OFF" position. Next I tried the side control to move down from "OFF" past "VOICE/MCW 243.0" and

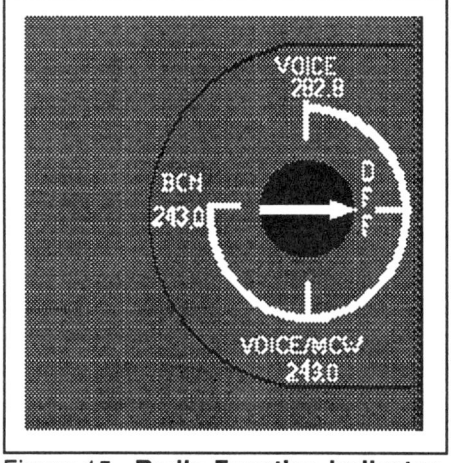

Figure 15. **Radio Function Indicator**

181

on to "BCN 243.0." This worked fine, but I still could not get the indicator to go up past "OFF" to "VOICE 282.8."

* * * * * *119

I then looked at the operating instructions again and noticed instruction II.C. said "DEPRESS IND. ARROW AND ROTATE." So I pressed in on the arrow indicator itself on the front of the radio as I attempted to rotate the knob on the side of the radio. This time I got the arrow to move all the way to "VOICE 282.8." I then pressed the "PUSH-TO-TALK" button and repeated: "Hello airplane. This is the *Haleakala*. Over."

There was an immediate and much less formal answer: "Hello. Are you injured?"

I had established radio contact! I answered I was not seriously injured, although I had bruises, lacerations, and some sunburn. I did not add that my arm and legs had been badly scraped sometime during the ordeal, and I had bled some from the wounds. I was lucky I had not attracted any sharks, particularly while I was so vulnerable to an attack!

---

[119]Before going on, the reader is invited to figure out what I had to do to get the radio working. The operating instructions shown as Figure 14 are printed to scale, white on black, and appear here very close to the actual appearance on the back of the radio. Figure 15 is a full-scale picture of the area on front of the radio which includes the function indicator. The arrow shown is painted on a black disk that turns with the frequency selector function knob switch on the side of the radio. The indicator arrow is raised about 1/16" from a 1/16" depression extending out to the white circle. The function knob (not shown) is a "thumb wheel" on the side of the radio that clicks into place when changed from setting to setting.

They asked what I needed, and I replied I needed water. "You should find water in the drum. Do you find the water?"

I took the top off of the drum again, opened the plastic bag and looked inside. I found a silver gray can with black printing that said "EMERGENCY DRINKING WATER." I replied: "Yes, I found the water."

"You should also find food. Do you find the food?"

I found several small cans of K-rations in the drum and replied: "Yes, I found some canned food. Is there a can opener here also?"

"Yes, do you find the can opener?"

I rummaged around in the plastic bag for a few seconds without finding it and, deciding to ignore it for the time being, I said: "I don't find it now, but I'm sure it's here."

They asked if I saw flares in the drum. I located them and said I had found them. They then wanted to know what else I needed. I replied: "Well, I need something for protection from the sun but I can use the parachute for a sunshade."

"You should also find a survival blanket in there. Do you find the survival blanket?"

I searched through the bag and found a small orange packet with "SURVIVAL BLANKET" written on it. "Yes I found it."

With my immediate needs answered I then asked: "Have you seen the rafts you dropped last night? I left my cat, Sadie, on one of the rafts. Did you see her?"

They told me that they had been searching for the rafts the whole time we've been here without finding any trace of them. After their last pass over the search area, they had decided to come up this way to make a quick search for the wreckage[120] before they had to depart.

This statement stunned me! I had assumed that they had located the rafts first and, having found I was not aboard any of them, then came looking for me here on the boat. I was not surprised they first looked for the rafts, but I was astonished they had not FOUND them.

My first decision as to what to do at dawn had been to swim for the rafts. My subsequent decision to abandon the rafts and commit to the swim for the boat was the difference in having just been located and being still lost. I simply could not believe they were unable to find the rafts![121]

The plane was already some distance off and flying away from me to the east when they said: "We cannot stay in the

---

[120]This is how I remember the conversation although they should have (wrongfully) assumed that the rafts and wreckage would be drifting as a group going together in the direction the wind and current took them. Of course, I knew that they were drifting apart and this knowledge may have biased my interpretation of what they said. They must have decided that after patrolling the expected position accounting for drift they flew up current toward the last reported position and located me even further up current. This is also the general direction they would have taken from the search site to Christmas Island.

MAC-38084 had reported the rafts spread over a mile and a half at dawn (see page 140), and the Coast Guard flight may have thus assumed that they had to ignore the EPIRB radio beacon with the wreckage in order to find the rafts now considerably down wind from their drop location. This would be consistent with a final pass toward the EPIRB signal on the wreckage on the way to Christmas Island. Even without the RDF equipment, the location of the EPIRB could be determined by its change in signal strength as the were flying the search pattern.

[121]Three rafts had been dropped the previous night apparently along with EPIRB locator radio beacons as I found out later, and the crew had been unable to find any of the rafts or radios!

184

area, we must leave immediately to refuel. A ship is under way and is expected to arrive on site at about twelve."

"Is that twelve midnight tonight or twelve noon tomorrow?"

"Midnight tonight."

After that I could make out only a few words of their transmission. It sounded something like:

... "RADIO" ... "HALF AN HOUR" ... "DISCOVER" ... "AIRPLANE" ...

But I could not understand the gist of the message. They were reaching the limit of my reception by this time, and I thought they might have said they wanted me to use the RADIO to keep checking in every HALF HOUR so they could DISCOVER any deterioration in my condition or to keep in contact with an AIRPLANE, so I said: "I could not understand your last transmission. Are you asking me to come up on this frequency and check in every half hour?"

They transmitted something back but all I understood was:

"NO" ... "AIRPLANE" ... and a few other garbled words.

By this time the plane was well out of sight, and I could hear nothing more from them. From the way they spoke of "airplane," I got the impression a different plane would be trying to contact me.

Radio operating instruction IV said: "QUIET OPERATION - EARPHONE" and I had noticed the earphone in a pouch on the strap of the radio. I took it out, plugged it in, and tried to see if I could hear the plane better with it.

However, reception with the earphone was no better than with the built-in speaker, so I unplugged it from the radio and put it back in the pouch. "Quiet operation" obviously meant "not disturbing to others" rather than "low-level signal reception."

Joy!

As soon as the Coast Guard plane saw me they immediately reported to the JRCC.

23 APR 0240Z (1540X) 00°25'N 164°59'W, 3:40 p.m.

Joy! CG-1414 had relocated the vessel with the survivor back aboard! Amazingly, after the brief one hour search was fruitless, the wreckage and survivor were located a very short time later, but only a few more minutes of on-scene time remained if CG-1414 was to be able to land at Christmas Island before dark. Any attempt to fly back to Honolulu would exceed the normal fuel supply allocation, endanger the plane and crew, and certainly force use of the required fuel reserves.

In spite of the lack of continuous coverage as originally planned to prevent losing contact with the wreckage, both MAC-38084 and CG-1414 had located the vessel shortly after arriving on the scene. Certainly a testimony to the skill of the SAR planning and execution, and I believe that my efforts also had something to do with their success.

23 APR 0249Z (1549X) 00°25'N 164°58.8'W, 3:49 p.m.

The few additional minutes CG-1414 could remain on scene had been enough to establish communications on the radio they dropped. After our very brief conversation, they started for Christmas noting the EPIRB was still working on both 121.5 and 243 MHz, and now also augmented by the hand held EPIRB/voice transmitter they had dropped.

23 APR 0254Z (1554X) 00°25'N 164°59'W, 3:54 p.m.

Immediately after departing and in route to a sunset landing, they radioed a brief sighting report synopsis. They reaffirmed that due to available daylight CG-1414 had to leave the scene immediately. While departing they had dropped a Datum Marker Buoy[122] on station set to a frequency of 240.6 MHz. They reported the vessel was capsized with one person on board between the two hulls and that he reported minor cuts and bruises but no physical problems. Communications were established on 282.8 MHz.

Without delay the JRCC briefed Elli on this latest and finally good news from CG-1414, including my report of only minor injuries.

After having landed safely at Christmas Island several hours later, CG-1414 wired the more detailed formal report.

---

[122]The Datum Marker Buoy is a radio beacon designed to drift along with flotsam (or whatever is to be marked) moving along with it in the ocean current and thereby maintaining a marker of its continually changing position.

Document 17.

23 APR 0645Z (2045W) 8:45 p.m. Telex (page 1 of 2).

FROM CG-1414 CHRISTMAS ISLAND (VIA KURE ISLAND)
TO JRCC HONOLULU HI
SUBJECT: DISTRESS SITUATION REPORT:
     S/V HALEAKALA SINKING

  1. SITUATION:

    A.   SUBJECT LOCATED AT POSITION 00-25N 164-59W
AT 230240Z. OWNER/OPERATOR IN GOOD CONDITION
WITH MINOR CUTS AND BRUISES, BOAT IS TOTALLY
INVERTED AND SEEMS TO BE RIDING WELL IN WATER. A
RADIO CAN CONTAINING PORTABLE RADIO, 14 PEN GUN
FLARES, 2 DAY/NIGHT FLARES, FOOD, WATER, SPACE
BLANKET, JELLY BEANS WERE DROPPED AND RECOVERED
BY MR. COLEMAN. COMMUNICATION WITH MR. COLEMAN
IS ON 282.8 MHZ. FREQUENCY 243.0 MHZ IS AVAILABLE
ON PORTABLE RADIO, HOWEVER, DUE TO DROWN OUT BY
VESSELS EPIRB, WHICH IS TRANSMITTING CONTINUOUSLY
ON 121.5 MHZ AND 243.0 MHZ, MR. COLEMAN WILL REMAIN
WITH LISTENING WATCH ON 282.8 MHZ.

    B.   DATUM MARKER BUOY DROPPED 0254Z ON
FREQUENCY 240.6 MHZ AT THE SAME POSITION.

    C.   WEATHER: 10 SCATTERED, WINDS 060 AT 10
KNOTS, SEAS 040 AT 3 FEET. VISIBILITY IS 20 MILES.

Rescue Preparations

When I was sure that the plane had gone I decided to
savor a drink of water and to make a full inventory of the

Document 18.
23 APR 0645Z (2045W) 8:45 p.m. Telex (page 2 of 2).

2. ACTION TAKEN:

    A.   1545W CG-1414 ON STATION, PROCEEDING DOWN VESSEL DEAD RECKONING DRIFT FOR 25 NAUTICAL MILES.

    B.   1620W COMMENCED EXPANDING SQUARE SEARCH AT LAST KNOWN POSITION.

    C.   1640W SUBJECT LOCATED VISUALLY IN POSITION 00-25N 164-59W BY OMEGA.

    D.   1649W DROPPED RADIO CAN/SUPPLIES. COMMUNICATIONS WERE ESTABLISHED.

    E.   1654W DROPPED DATUM MARKER BUOY ON FREQUENCY 240.6 MHZ.

    F.   1705W CG 1414 DEPARTED SCENE IN ROUTE CHRISTMAS ISLAND DUE TO AVAILABLE DAYLIGHT.

    G.   1857W CG 1414 ON DECK AT CHRISTMAS ISLAND.

3. FUTURE PLANS/RECOMMENDATIONS:

    A.   AFR-823 TO PROCEED IN ROUTE TO RELOCATE SUBJECT. MAINTAIN RADIO DIRECTION FINDING GEAR FOR 121.5 MHZ AND 243.0 MHZ AND ATTEMPT COMMUNICATIONS ON 282.8 MHZ. CONDUCT VISUAL SEARCH FOR NIGHT SIGNAL DEVICE.

    B.   NOAAS DISCOVERER PROCEEDING IN ROUTE TO RECOVER SUBJECT FROM SAILING VESSEL.

    C.   CG-1414 RECOVERED AT CHRISTMAS ISLAND.

4. SAR STATISTICS: 1 SORTIE FLOWN, 0.9 HOURS SEARCHED, APPROXIMATELY 8.3 HOURS FLOWN.

contents of my Easter basket before I made rescue preparations. I got out the can of water and looked for the can opener they had told me was in the drum.[123] When I was unable to locate it rapidly, I began another more careful search of the entire survival package before I remembered my knife. Steadying the can on top of the keel, I opened the marlin spike on the knife and plunged it twice into the top of the can. I immediately drank the entire can full of water in slow measured sips. I wondered if the Coast Guard had considered pop-top cans for survival rations.

The scattered squalls seemed to be getting closer, and the seas were building rapidly and had risen to over seven feet from trough to crest. An occasional wave was breaking high enough to splash over the top of the drum even though it was at a height of more than six feet from the surface of the ocean. I had put it up on the ladder as far as I could and further shielded the contents from the spray with my body and the lid of the drum.

Rummaging through the plastic bag I found the additional items shown. Two items intrigued me: The FOOD PACKET because no contents were listed, and I wondered what it contained. And the ACCESSORY PACKET; I wondered why they had sent me salt, cream substitute, and toilet paper? (There is plenty of salt available in the sea, there was no coffee or tea for the cream substitute, and bodily hygiene is easy when there is so much water for bathing.)

---

[123]As it turned out, there was no can opener to be found.

EMERGENCY DRINKING WATER: 2 more cans
PLASTIC SPOON
CAKE, CHOCOLATE: a small can of pound cake
SPAGHETTI: 10 ounce can with meat balls
7 SIGNALS, HAND FIRED MK 80 MOD 0: flares
LIGHT MARKER,DISTRESS: a small strobe light
SURVIVAL BLANKET: orange and silver sides, in pouch
B-2 UNIT: a can of crackers, cocoa beverage powder
MIXED FRUIT: a squashed can
FOOD PACKET, SURVIVAL AIRCRAFT, LIFE RAFT: 2 packets
SUN GLASSES: in plastic pouch
B-3 UNIT: can of crackers, candy
CHEESE SPREAD, CHEDDAR: 37 gram can of pimento flavored
    spread
SIGNALING MIRROR: approximately 4 by 6 inches with
    instructions
SMALL CORD: approximately 150 feet
BEACON SET, RADIO AN/URT-33 A: another EPIRB without voice
    capability
ACCESSORY PACKET: matches, chewing gum, toilet paper,
    instant coffee, cream substitute, sugar, salt

Figure 16 **Inventory of Supplies.**

Immediately after taking inventory I chose my dinner menu, the can of spaghetti with meat balls for the main course and the can of chocolate pound cake for dessert. Opening the can of spaghetti, I thought to myself: "I have had my jellybeans, and even if I don't have any colored eggs or turkey, this will be my own Easter Sunday dinner."

With the food that had probably been canned during World War II, I have never had an Easter dinner that tasted any better. The salty sea air always seems to make things taste better, but adding my hunger, fatigue, and exposure to the elements, this was certainly the most delicious spaghetti I ever ate.

When it was time for dessert, my mouth watered as I opened the can of chocolate cake, expecting a rich, moist devils food cake. Although I ate every crumb because I was hungry and certainly wasn't going to waste anything, I cannot recommend the dry tasteless cake even when shipwrecked. But, at least it provided nutrition. It really did not taste bad so much as simply having no flavor at all except for a hint of dry saw dust. I barely got it down, and eating it may have been a mistake after all because the dryness made me think of water again.

Since I had two more cans of water and I had been promised a ship at midnight, I decided to splurge with my second drink of water in nearly as many days. In case the ship could not find me, or in the unlikely event that the plane had meant midnight tomorrow, I still would have one can in reserve. The water I consumed would sustain me at least two more days at the very minimum. I knew that one 10-ounce can of water can sustain a person for one day, and I had not yet been overly dehydrated. In addition, I was confident that the Coast Guard could now find me again since I had the radio with the Mayday beacon frequency.

I was disappointed with my dessert, and considered having something better to serve as an

Document 19. Survival Food Instructions.

"INSTRUCTIONS: The food in this packet, especially developed for survival use, will be beneficial even when water supply is limited. When entirely consumed by one man in one day the packet will maintain survival efficiency. Items must not be allowed to get wet. Keep unused components in packet bag. Use twine (placed in the fold) to tie mouth of bag securely."

Easter treat. Looking through the drum again, I found the mysterious survival food packet on top. I could feel two hard lumps about the size of small candy bars in the packet. I decided to open this intriguing packet with the cryptic label: "FOOD PACKET, SURVIVAL AIRCRAFT, LIFE RAFT."
I wouldn't waste whatever I found, and I wanted to see just what they considered life raft survival rations. Inside were two square packets each about the size of a roll of lifesavers, containing hard candies in assorted fruit favors. With the candies was a printed sheet of paper, shown as Document 19.

These fruit flavored hard candies sounded like just the right thing for a real Easter Sunday dessert, and over the next hour or two I savored them carefully, one at a time. I realized that all kinds of hard candies are nonperishable if kept dry according to these instructions and that they provide the necessary energy supply for survival just like the jellybeans. I now include hard candy as survival rations along with tuna fish packed in water in aluminum cans.

Having satisfied my hunger and thirst, with a candy in my mouth to savor, it was time to prepare for rescue. I first relocated the packet of flares in the drum. Opening the packet revealed a set of seven flares in a plastic holder wrapped in a printed sheet of cardboard with instructions as shown as Document 20.

The instructions would be easy to follow except for one very crucial problem: *There was no projector with the flares!* "Oh, No! Not another can opener oversight!" I still had five shotgun shell type flares in my pocket that I also could not fire because

Document 20. Mini-flare Instruction Card.

OPERATING INSTRUCTIONS

1. PULL TRIGGER SCREW INTO ANGULAR (SAFETY) SLOT.
2. BEND PROTECTIVE TAB AWAY FROM SIGNAL IN BANDOLEER TO ALLOW ATTACHMENT OF PROJECTOR.
3. MATE PROJECTOR WITH SIGNAL AND ROTATE TO RIGHT UNTIL SIGNAL IS SEATED.
4. HOLD PROJECTOR, ARM FULLY EXTENDED, OVERHEAD.
5. GRIP PROJECTOR FIRMLY. WITH SNAPPING THUMB ACTION, PULL TRIGGER FROM SAFETY SLOT AND RELEASE INTO FIRING SLOT.
6. IF SIGNAL MISFIRES, AT LEAST ONE MORE ATTEMPT SHOULD BE MADE TO FIRE IT.
7. UNSCREW MISFIRED OR SPENT SIGNAL.

---

of the lack of a flare gun! There was only one thing to do; go through the drum again making a more careful second inspection to see if I had possibly missed a small pencil flare gun. The things found on this second inspection are listed as Figure 17.

The two items that I was looking for were the missing flare projector gun

TURKEY LOAF: a 5-3/4 ounce can
7 SIGNALS, HAND FIRED MK 80 MOD 0: flares with gun
SUN GLASSES: second pair in plastic pouch
JAM, APRICOT: a 1.5 ounce can
PARACHUTE CORD: approximately 20 feet

Figure 17 **Second Search Results.**

and the survival blanket to keep warm as the evening chill was in the air. Searching through the drum, I found a second pouch of flares and then the survival blanket. I took them out, folded the plastic bag down over all of the remaining things in the drum, put the blanket back on top, and restored the lid. When I opened the second pack of flares, success! This packet contained a pencil flare gun in addition to extra flares. Why would anyone pack flares in the drum without a flare gun attached to each bandoleer? But then why did I leave my own flare gun on the raft?

I fastened the pencil flare projector safely to the bandoleer of flares with the attached lanyard and tied the set to my harness to join the collection of things I considered essential to survival. I then reviewed the instructions on how to load the gun. Following the instructions, I loaded it leaving a flare ready on the projector. But, I left the gun un-cocked so it could not go off prematurely and then put the entire package in my pocket ready for the arrival of the rescue ship.

Even after the second search I still had not find everything in the drum. It also contained the items listed in the Figure.

```
1/4 INCH CHAIN: 12 feet with hook
2 INCH FOAM PAD: fit into the bottom of the
      drum covering the chain and with a
      second message: "IF YOU HEAR US
      TALK PUSH TO TALK"
```

Figure 18 **Items Not Inventoried.**

The chain and foam pad were missed because they were under the plastic bag lining the drum. The chain also served as ballast to keep the drum upright in the water as well as being useful survival material.

195

It was getting late in the evening, now time to deploy the small strobes in the most visible positions around the *Haleakala*. One strobe would be best placed on the other rudder.[124] With a piece of the cord from the survival drum I tied one small strobe to the outer side at the top of the rudder in a position that would be visible from all around the horizon with no obstructions on the right side of the *Haleakala* raft. I then returned to the left side and put my second small strobe on the outside of the other rudder. Now at least one of the two small strobes could be seen from any direction, and both strobes could be seen from nearly all directions except when one was shadowed by me, the other rudder, or the hull.

The sun was beginning to set as I climbed back up on my piece of broken ladder. I draped the lanyard of the large strobe over my shoulder and under my left arm, again positioning the strobe on my back. Now it too could be seen from nearly all quarters as I moved around. And as always, I kept it attached to my harness. I also tried to read the printing on one of the survival packets in the light of the strobe, but discovered that the printing on all of the survival packets was nearly invisible at dusk, being black lettering on a dark olive drab background. The strobe made it doubly hard to read anything including the time on my watch because of the intermittent very bright flash. Luckily there was nothing more I needed to read in the dark.

The sun had set; it would only be a few minutes before total darkness, and already there was a chill in the air. My watch

---

[124]This was the port rudder of *Haleakala* although it was now on the starboard side of the overturned boat. Because in the overturned position the rudder functioned more as a weather vane so it could be referred to as the "starboard vane."

showed it was more than two hours since the plane had departed. Although they did not want me to keep checking in every hour, I decided to try and raise someone on the radio. I called twice waiting between calls but received no answer, as expected.

I knew transmission takes a lot more power than reception, and I did not want to waste the battery with fruitless calls. It is doubtful that the battery would last for over an hour or so of transmission although it should last for many days or even weeks on reception. With forethought, I left the radio tuned to receive on 282.8 MHz, took off the earphone, adjusted the volume so the static could be heard without picking up the radio, and put the lanyard around my neck so the radio sat on my chest while still fastened to the harness.[125]

AFR-823

Mechanical and electronic problems seemed to plague this SAR mission from its earliest hours. Going back many hours, Flight 551 said they were unable to detect the EPIRB; problems had delayed the takeoff of CG-1414 requiring a return to base before it finally got underway a second time to the

---

[125]The earphone was not really considered essential for communication, so I did not include it separately in the collection of critical survival gear attached to my harness. Of all of the things I tried to save, only the earphone got lost. It was there every time I wanted to use it. But it dropped out of its pocket and went overboard sometime without my notice.

Mayday site; and even on site, CG-1414 continued to have RDF problems. Even before the Coast Guard plane had made its initial contact, the Air Force 6594th Group also reported mechanical difficulties.

23 APR 0200Z (1600W) Hickam Air Force Base, 4:00 p.m.

Just as CG-1414 was beginning the initial expanding square search pattern at the equator, the Air Force 6594th Group reported the relief C-130 was not operational; it too was down with mechanical trouble. One more (last) plane was available, and the crew was transferring to the secondary aircraft. The transfer and pre-flight checkout would take at least an hour meaning that five o'clock that afternoon (0300Z) would be the earliest departure time for the new flight AFR-823, the replacement for the plane originally intended to relieve CG-1414.

Hickam was asked to advise the JRCC of the progress in getting the second Air Force plane ready, but it was clear that continuous air coverage was now out of the question before dawn the next day. By then CG-1414 should be joined by another C-130 from McClellan Air Force Base, and, with the secondary plane from the 6594th then joining the mission, continuous air coverage would finally be possible a day later than planned. The deployment of all of these resources partly depended on the success of the 25-minute search then underway by CG-1414.

Joy! There must have been a cheer echoing in the Search and Rescue Center when CG-1414 reported they relocated the survivor. They had dropped survival supplies, established radio communication with the survivor, and he appeared calm and well. The need for additional SAR resources to support the mission which was a major problem a few moments before had eased greatly. It was now apparent at the SAR Center that rescue was probable without additional resources beyond those already committed.

The Air Force C-130 was still needed to aid *Discoverer* in locating the distressed vessel. Without an RDF capability for the EPIRB frequencies, the ship would have to get within flare sighting distance to make a night pickup. A C-130 overflight, timed to arrive as the SAR surface vessel reached the scene, would assure electronic vectoring as well as provide a visual sighting capability over the large area which is visible from a medium altitude overflight.

Document 21.

22 APR 0348Z (1748W) 5:48 p.m. Telex

FROM JRCC HONOLULU HI
TO COGARD COMMSTA HONOLULU HI

SUBJECT: DISTRESS CANCELLATION BROADCAST IN ACCORDANCE WITH INTERNATIONAL TELEGRAPHIC UNION REGULATIONS ON 500KHZ, 2182KHZ UPON RECEIPT.

QUOTE:

THE SAILING VESSEL HALEAKALA HAD BEEN LOCATED IN POSITION 00-25N 164-59W AND IS RECEIVING ASSISTANCE FROM US MILITARY ASSETS AND THE NOAA VESSEL DISCOVERER.

SIGNED US COAST GUARD HONOLULU HI

UNQUOTE:

Further resources beyond the *Discoverer* and the C-130 seemed to be unnecessary, and CG-1414 would still be on Christmas Island available for a morning flight if major new problems developed overnight. The situation appeared under control, and it was time to cancel the distress notice to mariners.

Chilling Wind

Unaware of the activities at the SAR Center, I had finished my rescue preparations. In the short time while I was settling down for the night, the expected darkness suddenly descended. With darkness came a chilling wind, and I shivered in soaking wet clothes.

I kept looking for the ship on the horizon before realizing that I was clearly getting overanxious. The Coast Guard plane had said the ship would arrive about midnight. I figured even if she were very early, she would not arrive before 11 p.m., an hour before it was due. I decided that the very earliest I should try to raise her on the radio would be about 10 o'clock. That would be the time to look for her in earnest; she should be quite invisible over the horizon until then.

In the hours before that I planned to "just look around," particularly for the lights from the rafts. Since the plane had not seen the rafts, I knew I would have very little chance of seeing them hours later from my vantage point so close to the water. But knowing Sadie was still aboard one of those life rafts, I

200

continued to search the horizon hoping to see a flash from a raft strobe.

I now had all three of my strobes flashing. I was most confident in the largest and chose it to be the one to remain tied to me at all times. I knew that it would outlast the small ones because of its much larger battery. And, I also knew that its battery was fresh because I had replaced it just before leaving Pago Pago and had rechecked the voltage that fateful day.

Although the plane had not told me from which direction the ship would arrive, I had been concentrating on the south southwest horizon, expecting the ship to come from there. Somewhere in my subconscious I thought she would also come from the direction I had sailed, namely from the direction of Pago Pago, American Samoa. This intuitive direction was opposite of the most likely direction.

It was more probable the rescue ship would come from exactly the other direction, namely from the direction of Hawaii rather than Pago Pago. There was a lot more ocean traffic between the islands in that direction than between the South Central Pacific islands. Most likely, Christmas Island at about 400 nautical miles to the northeast and Palmyra Island about the same distance to the north were the islands from which help would be coming.

For a couple of hours more I continued to look just south of west for the rafts with Sadie although I fully realized that this was illogical since our distance apart would now be over twenty miles. However, this was "free time," not yet "search time," which I planned for later.

The seas had built up higher than they had been all day. The waves that broke over the leading edge of the wing every ten minutes or so were getting large enough to knock me off of my ladder. With the sun down I was also getting quite cold from the wetness and the night wind now blowing over twenty knots. As I shivered in the chill, I thought about protection from the cold and opened the drum to get the pouch labeled "Survival Blanket."

The survival blanket was inside a pouch about the size of a book. It unfolded to about three by six feet and was made of plastic about the thickness of a household trash bag. It had a shiny aluminum color on one side and a very bright fluorescent orange on the other. I wrapped it around my shoulders and pulled it tight across my back, over the life vest, and around my waist. It afforded some protection and comfort from the chill.

The next high wave hit me and tore the blanket in two! The smaller piece disappeared in the swirling water. Before I could react, another wave hit me and tore another piece out of the remaining blanket. During the following lull in the waves, I climbed all the way up the ladder and onto the keel between the rudder and the prop. Then I took the remaining pieces of the shredded plastic blanket and stuffed them under my T-shirt. This gave me some extra protection but not enough to keep me from constant shivering.

The survival blanket had been a complete failure for me! I could easily tear the flimsy plastic between my fingers. It is possible the plastic had deteriorated in the years since it was first put in the drum.[126]

---

[126]It has been suggested that the survival blanket included in the emergency supplies canister was a NASA-developed survival blanket who's objectives were high thermal protection-to-weight and not protection from wind and waves.

(continued...)

With the survival blanket essentially useless, I reverted to my original plan of using the parachute to keep warm. This met with little more success. The nylon was so thin the water and air went right through it. Although it provided little warmth, I continued to keep it over my shoulders. I had to get my mind off of my discomfort.

With the strobes in place, the radio on and set to maximum volume, and the flares ready, I had done everything I needed to do prior to the arrival of the ship. Now I could think of Elli and our poor Sadie. These thoughts kept my mind off of my cold and wet discomfort, and for awhile I tried to forget I was stranded in the middle of the ocean. Elli had once said in jest: "Don't come back without Sadie." Now after having taken full responsibility for Sadie, she was adrift on a raft and would certainly die if not rescued. I was mourning her loss and dreaded having to tell Elli.

Sadie had been great company while sailing, although a couple of times she had taken my breath away with her fearless antics. During the day she liked to sleep over the rushing water nestled in a fold of the Genoa sail, which was lashed to the net between the bows. I gently brought her back in the cabin

---

[126](...continued)

If the lack of strength of this material is inherent, and not due to deterioration while stored, then it does not seem appropriate to use in a mid ocean survival situation. Now even ordinary throw-away plastic grocery bags are substantially stronger when new than the (old?) survival blanket turned out to be. Modern plastics, such as mylar probably would have stood up to severe pounding of the sea and can be easily silvered for thermal protection. The few ounces of mylar would be no problem in a canister where a length of chain was used for ballast.

whenever I saw her out on the sail although she was relatively safe there. If she should slip, she could always grab onto the sail material with her claws before going overboard.

Once, however, Sadie really scared me by walking out onto the slick, painted, aluminum compression beam between the bows while we were underway. She could have easily slipped from it into the ocean as she had done several times as a kitten. I was inside the main cabin when I saw her there staring at the water rushing back between the hulls. I had to hold my breath to keep from running out on deck and yelling at her. I did not want to startle her and risk having her react by falling into the ocean. With only me aboard, it would be quite a problem getting her back out of the water.

I frantically planned what to do if she did fall in. First I would throw a floating cushion or two in the water for her to swim and cling to, and the man overboard pole to mark the spot. Then I would go through the full "man" overboard drill to recover her. As I stood there deciding what to do first, she calmly climbed down from the compression beam. I went forward, retrieved her, and petted her as I took her below. She never knew she was in danger nor the fright it had given me.

The likelihood of having to abandon Sadie distressed me. She could not survive without help, and I grieved her loss. but, at least now I was sure I was going back to Elli, myself. I knew the Coast Guard must have contacted her when I first gave them her telephone number. But, although the first news she received must have been a shock, the later reports, while I was floating all but invisible in the water, must have been about the worst possible information. Would she now know the latest news? If the afternoon Coast Guard plane had reported in, and it surely must have by this time, she must now know that I am "safe" on the *Haleakala* raft.

Cloudy Halo

As I was thinking of Elli, a bright cloudy halo at the horizon caught my eye! The light was not moving and was more diffuse than the "moving star" of the night before. I pushed the button to turn on the little light on my watch, and though it was not a very effective light, I was able to verify it was not yet ten o'clock. I was not expecting the rescue ship for another couple of hours, but I was definitely looking at a diffused light in the clouds that could not be a celestial body.

As I watched I thought I could see the light move! I watched it for several minutes longer as I took the bandoleer of flares out of my pocket and readied the pencil flare gun. I wanted to see which way the light was moving before I fired the flare.

The halo was in the south southwest as I had somehow expected. Although I could not see a ship, I figured that I was seeing the glow of a ship's lights on the clouds above her. I pulled the firing pin back and seated it in the cocked position as I watched for more movement at the horizon. The halo was so far away that it was hard to tell if the light was indeed moving. But, in a few minutes I could tell from the changing bearings that the light was moving northward with noticeable speed. The light looked more and more like a ship that would pass to the north of me if she maintained her present course. Satisfied I was seeing a ship's lights I raised my arm and fired my first flare.

After firing the flare I continued to watch the moving light. From the change in relative bearing, I guessed they would have missed me by only a couple of miles if I had not signaled. The glow in the clouds seemed to slow down and then came to an apparent stop. From the large size of the glow and the slow movement, I felt confident that it must be caused by a ship that had seen my flare and had changed course toward me, with the constant bearing making it appear to have stopped. Although they could have changed course directly away from me, I thought that very unlikely right after I had fired a flare. But I wanted to make sure they had seen my flare and remembered the radio, which I should have tried first.

The radio was around my neck, still switched to receive voice on 282.8 MHz. Nearly constant background static crackled from the speaker, while I could hear nothing from the ship. Turning the volume all the way up only made the static louder.

"Hello ship. This is Charley Coleman of the *Haleakala*. Over."

A loud but unintelligible voice came back. I turned the volume down and answered: "Ship, I hear your transmission. You are loud but garbled. I cannot understand what you said. Over."

There was a long pause before they answered. Then a loud and this time very clear voice, which sounded different from the previous voice, said: "Hello. How are you?"

I had contact with the ship! I was saved! Before long I should be safely aboard! Rescue looked certain, and I was

206

overjoyed, even though I was not yet aboard. I began to see their lights beneath the glow.

"I'm fine but a little cold. I can now see your lights quite clearly on the horizon. I have been watching the glow in the clouds over you for several minutes. You are now south southwest of me. It looked like you were going to pass to the north of me until I fired the flare. Did you see the flare and can you see my strobes?"

"We saw a flare but we have not yet seen your strobes. We want to get a better fix on you."

While I was talking to the ship I also noticed some lights from an airplane in the opposite direction. It was quite high and far away. However, the airplane was not heading directly for me so I told the ship: "I see an airplane, too."

"We are the airplane. We are an Air Force Hercules."

Hercules

The Hercules had caught me by surprise. While I thought I was talking to the ship, I was actually talking to the plane. This was the reason that there was some confusion when I tried to tell the "ship" its relative bearing.

The plane was at a high altitude and maybe over ten miles away. I assume they had come in at such high altitude to pick up the EPIRB transmissions from the greatest distance, although that would make it very difficult to pick me out visually or even with flashing strobes. However, with radio contact first established, visual contact should be quite easy using RDF and the help I could give them. Turning my attention to the plane, I said: "In that case, Hercules, I can also see a ship southwest of me."

The plane responded: "We can see the ship; that is the NOAA ship *Discoverer*. They spotted your flare and think they can now see your strobes. We are going to fly over you to verify your position. Would you give us a mark when we are right above you?"

I said I understood that I was to give them a mark at their highest position. However, I also told them it did not look to me as if they were going to fly directly over but rather to the east of me. Although I could not see the actual airplane in the dark, I could see their navigation lights clearly. Relying only on the appearance of the lights, I could not be certain of either their altitude or distance. But I guessed they were at least 10,000 feet high, probably higher, and still over five miles away.

From the time I had first spotted them, they had been high in the northeast sky and flying south. Now, as I watched, they descended, turned more toward the north, and flew parallel to me. Descending further, they turned back toward the south and flew level over and ahead of me. When they reached the highest angle, I said: "Mark! You are to the east northeast of me at an angle of about 80 degrees, or 10 degrees east northeast of my zenith." I tried to be quite formal and precise so that there could be no confusion.[127]

---

[127]The reader can now appreciate how hard it must be to spot an object in the ocean even with strobe lights and with detailed communication between aircraft and the surface.

208

They said they had spotted me, could now see my strobes, and were relaying my position to the *Discoverer*. I told them I understood, but I silently wondered why they had to relay my position since the ship could accurately tell my position from the messages I had been transmitting. The ship too was now clearly in line-of-sight and should easily be able to pick up my UHF radio signal from that distance. So I asked: "Can't the *Discoverer* copy our conversation?"

Another surprise! "No. The *Discoverer* cannot receive this frequency. We are here to serve as radio relay for you, and we are now in contact with them. They are going to come up to within a mile or so and launch an inflatable boat. They will then come over and pick you up in the Zodiac. They can now see your strobes, and expect it will take them about another half an hour before they are in position to launch the Zodiac. Do you want us to relay anything to them?"

I thought of asking if I should switch back to 243.0 MHz from 282.8 MHz so the ship could hear me too, assuming (incorrectly) they could pick up the international air distress frequency. However, there seemed to be no point in doing that since I knew the EPIRB aboard would interfere with my reception if not also with my transmission. The plane in position overhead would be able to relay anything I wanted to say, and there was nothing to communicate other than my location and their plans, which had already been sent. I guessed it would be another half an hour or so even after they launched the Zodiac before they would actually reach me.

"Hercules, I have nothing more to relay now, but in the meantime, have you seen the lights on the life rafts from up there? I left my cat, Sadie, on one of the rescue rafts you dropped me last night. They should now be to the west southwest of me about 20 or 25 miles away. There were a lot of small lights in the water and one or two strobes with the rafts. They should be visible from the air. Can you see them?"

They replied that they had not seen the rafts and could not see them now in that direction. They added they would not be able to see them that far away. Then they asked about Sadie.

We had a rather long conversation about Sadie Thompson while they circled and the ship approached. I told them how I swam for a raft and put Sadie aboard, how I had then been separated from the rafts and Sadie, and how I had been able to save myself by swimming back to *Haleakala*. I wanted to save her life too if I could.

The men in the Hercules seemed amazed at my story and very understanding and compassionate about Sadie. They understood my loss and promised they would go on and look for the rafts once I was safely aboard the *Discoverer*. The direction in which I thought the rafts had drifted was the same general direction they were going to fly anyhow, and they promised to keep an eye out for lights from the rafts as they flew over the ocean. They would report to the ship if they could find anything at all.

While we talked about Sadie, the ship continued to come closer. I could now make out the form all ablaze with lights. It still had a large distinctive halo in the clouds above, the same glow I had first seen from afar. The halo apparently was made by search lights on the ship deliberately turned upward to illuminate the clouds, probably so I would see them from the greatest distance. I could now clearly see that the ship was

210

heading directly for me and could make out details of the superstructure.

I continued my conversation with the Hercules while the ship neared until it was approximately a mile or so away. When the ship hove-to it was still too far for me to see the activity aboard. The Hercules informed me the ship was deploying the inflatable and that they would be over shortly. I wondered if they would have any trouble with the Zodiac in the seas now running well over nine feet. Although a Zodiac is unsinkable, these waves could toss it around rather violently. Whoever came over after me should have quite a ride.

Lights Approaching

Finally, I knew rescue was near when I saw lights approaching. A hand-held spotlight shone in my direction, and I could tell the Zodiac was close although the height of the waves obscured the boat and occupants. In the last couple of hundred yards, they turned the light on themselves. I could see what appeared to be three men wearing orange life jackets.

As they approached I unshackled the parachute from the drum of survival supplies which was still fastened to my harness. I left the parachute tied to the prop shaft. The drum itself would not be a problem, in fact it floated and could be used to support a swimmer. I wanted to keep all of the contents of my

Easter basket, but I thought the parachute might get in the way of the rescue.[128]

I turned off the radio and stuffed it in my pocket, still keeping it also attached to my harness by the lanyard. Then I climbed down from my ladder and waited as the Zodiac came up to the stern. The roar of the sea and the outboard drowned out all conversation and I had to shout to them that there were jagged nails sticking out where the boarding ladder had been torn off and they might hole the inflatable. They then stood off a few feet while I shouted an explanation and pointed out where the nails were. I said I could come up over the hull and down into their boat on the other side. They agreed and came around to the left as I climbed back up the ladder to come down on the outside of the hull.

The seas had continued to rise since sundown and were now so high that as the tallest waves passed, the inflatable rose up on the crest and fell back down a total of about ten feet or so. There was even some danger the Zodiac might get caught under the edge of the *Haleakala*. We all decided this maneuver was not going to work in such choppy seas.

I suggested that I could get down in the water and they could pick me up from there. They said they would rather attempt coming up onto the stern anyway trying to avoid the nails. A Zodiac is made of rather heavy gauge reinforced plastic

---

[128]Although I very much wanted to keep the drum, now my only possession in the world, I would have abandoned it if it jeopardized my rescue in any way. In retrospect, I wish I had kept the parachute too. It would not have been hard to carry and would have been a colorful souvenir.

material, and they could probably have hit the nails rather hard without punching a hole through it.

They were still being tossed around quite a bit by the waves, and the coxswain stood-off timing his approach. Then he rode up on a wave and put the bow up on the stern. I thrust my drum aboard, still tied to me, and quickly pulled myself on amid a number of helping hands. The next wave came over the leading edge of the wing, swept down the length, and washed us all off of the trailing edge of the wing bottom. There were smiles all around and hand shakes from the three young men. I later found out that all were officers of the ship who had volunteered to come out on the rescue party to pick me up.

One of them had a hand-held radio much like the one I had, and he was in communication with the ship. He had it to his ear and was talking to them when he turned and said to me: "The airplane has requested that you turn off the EPIRB. They are still receiving it."

I reached for the radio in my pocket and checked it to see if I had somehow pushed the function knob too far to "BCN" instead of "OFF." The radio was indeed off and I replied: "I have turned off this EPIRB, but the EPIRB on the boat is still working."

There was a long pause while the message was relayed first to the ship and then to the airplane. It did not occur to me at the time to simply turn my radio back on and talk directly with the airplane. Then the radioman said: "They ask you to please turn off the one on the boat."

"It is a couple of feet under water and inaccessible inside the boat. You could turn it off with divers but we can't get at it from the surface."

213

After the message had been passed to the ship and on to the plane, they responded to the ship and the ship relayed back to the radioman and he to me: "Thanks, we thought the signal was from the hand-held you were using to talk to us (the Hercules)."

The Zodiac crew told me they had one more thing to do before they took me back—mount a radar reflector. We went back around the boat, and in the bouncing seas they were somehow able to throw a line over the rudder and lash a radar reflector to it. With the reflector in place, we headed for the ship still lying hove-to about a mile off.

As we were nearing the ship the rescue party passed out crash helmets and gave me one: "Would you put this on please?"

"Sure, but why?"

They explained the ship was going to pick us up using a "scoop." In these confused seas we would bang around a little as they lifted us out of the water, and the helmet was to protect my head. I would see what they meant when we got there. I thought to myself: "After all I've been through I'm not going to worry about a banged head." But I said nothing and quietly fastened the helmet on my head.

As we came alongside the ship, the scoop, an aptly named cage-like affair, was already in the water waiting for us. We motored into it using the outboard, and we all grabbed the sides to steady ourselves. The crane on deck was immediately engaged picking up the entire scoop, Zodiac, crew, and passenger, then quickly setting it all down on deck.

I was so deliriously happy at this time that I don't remember exactly what happened next, but I am told nearly the

214

entire ship's complement of officers and crew were waiting on deck and gave a huge cheer as the Zodiac touched the deck.

Aboard *Discoverer*

My knees buckled as I climbed out of the Zodiac and stepped aboard *Discoverer*. Without realizing it I had been driving myself so hard and living on so much adrenaline that the first moment I felt absolutely safe, I could hardly keep standing. The gentle pitching of the large ship in the ten foot seas almost knocked me off my feet even though I had been scrambling all over *Haleakala* for over two weeks since leaving Pago Pago. It was as if I had never been to sea and didn't know how to stand on a moving deck. The motion of three hundred foot *Discoverer* hove-to into the wind, was much more gentle than the motion of the relatively small *Haleakala* that I had just left. On surprisingly wobbly legs, I crossed the deck from the davit to the companionway leading below.

Several more men in khaki uniforms were standing at the companionway waiting for me. One appeared to me to be in charge so I asked him: "Are you the skipper?"

"No, I am the Operations Officer [Lieutenant Gary Lagerloef]. Would you like to speak to the skipper?"

"Yes," I said, and another officer who had been standing behind and to the right, came up to identify himself: "I'm Captain Robert Ganse."

"Can you contact my wife in Honolulu and tell her I'm safe? The Coast Guard in Honolulu has the phone number where she can be reached."

"We'll contact her. Is there anything else?"

I then proceeded to explain about Sadie. Now that I was safe and Elli would soon know that I had been rescued, Sadie had become my primary concern. I told him that Sadie was on one of the rafts, that I had gotten separated from her, and that there were lights on the rafts and in the water nearby. Had they seen them? He told me they had had lookouts posted for several hours, and they had seen nothing else in the water until I fired the flare. He then asked me the condition of the *Haleakala*.

I told him she had been holed and that her watertight integrity had been destroyed on the port side. I asked if he could right *Haleakala* and bring her aboard the *Discoverer*. He explained their strongest crane would be unable to lift her or even turn her right side up. Did I have anything of special value aboard?

I told him all of my possessions had been aboard, although what had not been emptied out as flotsam was surely soaked in seawater. The most valuable single thing I could think of at the moment that should also still be salvageable was the SATNAV. Since it was fully waterproof,[129] it should be in

---

[129]I do not know to what depth the SATNAV could be taken before it would leak but it was surely intact at the few feet below the surface where it lay. It was enclosed in a substantial steel case and sealed with o-rings for protection against water penetration. The controls were by means of an elastic diaphragm type switch plate so the "buttons" would certainly be "pushed" by the water pressure. However, no pattern of pushing buttons could harm the internal

(continued...)

perfect shape if he sent a diver for it. Perhaps he could send a diver into the boat to see if there were anything else salvageable left aboard. He said: "We'll see. First we have to determine if you have to be evacuated. If so, we will have to proceed to a medical evacuation rendezvous at Christmas Island."

I explained that I didn't think I would have to be evacuated because I felt in pretty good shape. I said this even as I held tightly onto the stanchion for support. He pointed out the decision should be made by their doctor, who was ready to examine me in sick bay. With this, I was introduced to Terry, the ship's Medical Technician and asked to go with him to sick bay.

I agreed but asked again if they would look for Sadie, if I didn't have to be evacuated, and added where I thought the rafts had drifted. Somewhat, but not completely in jest he said he normally did not permit pets aboard but would make an exception for Sadie. They would be going back in that general direction if I did not need medical evacuation, and they would keep a lookout for the rafts on the way back.

Having received assurance they would look for Sadie, I turned to go below. I put my arm around Terry's shoulders relying on his help although I am a lot larger and heavier than he. He helped me down the companionway ladder, across the lower aft deck, and toward the sick bay. I was still carrying my

---

[129](...continued)

circuitry although the stored values might be useless. Finally, shorting out the power leads might discharge the internal battery back-up but would not otherwise hurt the device. It is possible that the shorting of the battery leads would not discharge the internal battery if battery lead reversal protection was built into the unit.

orange survival drum and he suggested I put it down. I gave the drum to one of the crew to keep for me. At his further suggestion I also took off my life jacket and harness with all of the attached survival gear. Since I had been relying on them for survival, I had a long moment's hesitation before I took them off.

He wrapped a warm blanket around my shoulders as we entered the ship from the weather deck. Even wrapped in the blanket, I shivered as we proceeded forward along the companionway toward sick bay. The air conditioning further chilled me because of my bare legs and skimpy, soaked clothes. I certainly must have been a sight—bruised, scraped, sunburned, and shivering—as I headed for my medical examination.

As we walked through the aft marine laboratory area toward sick bay, we were followed by two ship's officers. One of them turned out to be Dr. Leonard Bachman, the Chief Surgeon of NOAA. A NOAA ship normally has only one medical technician to help maintain the health of the crew aboard. On unusually long and extended cruises, as this one happened to be, a doctor is also assigned aboard. In addition, to keep in touch with the conduct of his field operations, the Chief Surgeon himself periodically accepts one of these shipboard assignments. Thus, by lucky coincidence, not only did the *Discoverer* have a doctor aboard, but the doctor was the head of the entire NOAA medical service.

Immediately upon arrival in sick bay I had a brief but thorough physical examination. Dr. Bachman monitored my heart, listened to my chest, and took my temperature. He examined my bruises, lacerations, and sunburn. Even wrapped in a blanket, I was still shivering hard from the cool air and my reaction to exposure, but a hot warm bath had been drawn for me while I was being examined.

As the doctor begin his examination Terry asked if there was anything I wanted. I told him I could sure use a cup of hot coffee. In a few moments, he brought me a steaming cup. It was just the right thing to warm me, and it tasted delicious.

Then the phone rang and Terry relayed that they had my wife on a radio phone patch and they were going to patch the call through to me.

The phone rang again in a few minutes, and this time Terry said: "They can't get the patch working through to the sick bay phone, but she's on the line waiting. Do you feel able to go up and take her call in the radio room?"

"Sure. Just show me the way."

Wrapped in a couple of fresh dry blankets and with Terry leading the way, we wound our way up through the inside of the ship to the radio room. On the way up, we passed a door labeled "Bridge - Authorized Personnel Only" but we turned the opposite direction, went a short distance and entered the radio shack. The radioman had the radio/phone patch all ready so I could talk to Elli in Honolulu.

My first concern was to reassure Elli that I was OK. Now rescued and well taken care of aboard a large ship everything was alright now.

Then I had to tell her about Sadie. I told her that both the airplane and the ship were going to look for the rafts with Sadie but that she was adrift with little hope. This news saddened her, as it did me. Her happiness that I was safe far outweighed the uncertainty about Sadie.

219

I asked: "Are you still going to Los Angeles for your birthday or will you be there when we get in? Over."

"Of course not, silly. I'll be here when the ship docks. Over."

Someone on frequency, evidently one of the ham operators who had established the radio phone patch added: "No, I don't think she is going to fly away now."

Since I would have still been at sea between Pago Pago and Honolulu on her birthday, Elli had planned to fly to Los Angeles to celebrate the occasion with friends. I was obviously not thinking too clearly when I asked whether she still planned to go. Both the urgency of letting her know that I was safe and the excitement of being safe aboard a ship muddled my thoughts. At that moment, talking to her on the radio made me realize how much I really missed her. At that moment I though of how my demise would have taken her away from me as much as the other was around.

After the call I was escorted back to sick bay and a waiting warm bath. Again Terry asked if I wanted anything else, maybe something to eat. I had developed quite an appetite again despite my World War II spaghetti dinner before dark. "Yes, I'd like some more coffee and maybe something to eat, but I should be able to go to the galley myself to get it after I finish my bath."

There was a knock at the door and Larry Murray, the Chief Survey Technician, came in with an armful of clothes. "You'll probably need these. We realized you don't have any other clothes and what you are wearing is soaked. Here are some dry things we[130] have for you." With that he gave me a complete change of clothes down to and including socks and sandals.

It was past midnight, now Monday, the day after Easter local time. After my hot bath and second cup of coffee, I was ready to get dressed in Larry's warm, dry presents and go looking for the galley.

Terry led me down the companionway to the crew mess. The man Terry escorted must have really looked like a "survivor" as he continued holding on to the rail along the bulkhead as he walked unsteadily the whole way to the galley. Still rather shaky, the survivor look was reinforced by the blanket still over my shoulders to keep me warm.

Several crew members were in the mess when we got there, and the Chief Mess Stewart personally made me a midnight breakfast of ham and eggs, toast and coffee. It tasted wonderful. I had a couple more cups of coffee for warmth, rehydration, and to settle my nerves. (I found that a warm cup of coffee helped me get back to sleep on the few occasions that I had insomnia.) Terry led a now more steady survivor back to sick bay where one of the berths had already been prepared. He gave me some magazines to read and left so that I could settle down and go to sleep.

But sleep would not come easily.

---

[130]I later learned the "we" he spoke of was himself, and he had given me his own clean clothes. I was and will remain thankful for his kind and thoughtful act.

Search for Sadie

I thumbed through one of the magazines without really reading anything and realized that in spite of my fatigue, I could not sleep while there was still a chance that Sadie might also be saved. Although I had now been without sleep for two nights and was still worn out by my long swim and exposure to sun and cold, I worried about the search for Sadie. I wanted to do something more to help rescue her. On my trip to the radio room, I had learned some of the layout of the ship, and I remembered the door to the bridge. So, quietly slipping out of sick bay, I started for the bridge.

I wound around up the stairs inside the ship until I was again at the door marked: "Bridge - Authorized Personnel Only." I knocked on the door.

"Come in."

I opened the door and came out into the very dim red glow of the bridge night lights. Several officers and crew were there, although I could not make them out until my eyes adapted to the darkness. They, of course, knew immediately who I was. Those who had not been out on deck to see me come aboard surely knew my description. They asked how I was feeling and if I couldn't sleep.

I started to tell them about Sadie and that I had come to the bridge to look out for her.

"We know about Sadie. We have just finished a couple of hours of patrol through the area you gave for the life rafts, and have kept our lookout watches posted since we picked you up and just took them down about twenty minutes ago. We have looked for the rafts and Sadie for the entire time since we picked you up but have not seen any of them." I was rather upset by the tragic news that Sadie would not be rescued.[131]

In the days aboard the *Discoverer* immediately following my rescue, I gave up hope for the rescue of Sadie and mourned her loss, as pet owners the world over can appreciate. I thought of the good times we had had and the good company she had been.

Word of the loss of Sadie had spread throughout the ship, and many offered their sympathy. One morning at breakfast, Robert Pitman, the research biologist aboard, came up to me

---

[131]A valiant effort had been made to save Sadie Thompson. Although I'm sure that none of the searches could be officially called a "search for a cat," nevertheless, three independent searches had been made for the life raft with Sadie aboard:

1. The Coast Guard Search and Rescue flight that found me and dropped the survival supplies had made their initial search hunting for the life rafts assuming I was aboard one of them before giving up and taking one last quick look for the overturned *Haleakala* on the way back to Christmas Island.
2. The Air Force plane that had served as spotter aircraft and radio relay promised me they would look for the rafts on their flight south after I had been rescued.
3. The *Discoverer* had devoted several hours of lookout time searching for lights on the life rafts with Sadie along the ship's course back to her next oceanic research station.

In spite of all of these searches, the rafts had not been found, and I knew Sadie was lost at sea.

and said: "I understand that you think that Sadie is lost. I didn't realize that you were worried about the *survival* of your cat."

He proceeded to explain to me about how tenacious cats are and that there was a good chance she would survive. What she needed most was water and then food.

For water, she would have the frequent light rain squalls that were common at that time. In fact there had been light squalls the night I left her on the raft as well as the night I was picked up. She should have had water right away, and it didn't take much water to keep a cat alive.

And, food should be no problem either. There are flying fish out at night, and the first one would keep her going until the next one landed on the raft. I remembered we had quite a few come aboard *Haleakala* while we were sailing. Sadie did taste one or two although she preferred her dry cat food. He told me that on this trip they even had flying fish land on the Boat Deck of the *Discoverer*, a height of over 25 feet from the surface of the water. Although I probably would never see Sadie again he was sure that she would survive on rain water and flying fish."

I felt much better with Bob's analysis.[132]

---

[132] I will never know for sure, but there is at least a reasonable chance that Sadie lived on the rain water and flying fish until her bright orange raft got close enough to an island where a fisherman or sailor would came out to claim the raft.

Sadie was not wearing her identification collar when I left her. I always removed her collar when we sailed so that she would not get it hooked on anything. If the raft were to wash ashore before it was found by anyone, and the life raft surely would eventually wash ashore somewhere, then she could make her life among the animals and birds on whatever island or continent she ultimately landed.

(continued...)

Mission Conclusion

The Operations phase of the SAR mission to rescue the survivor of the foundered vessel ended when Dr. Bachman determined medical evacuation was not necessary. Otherwise Operations would have continued until the survivor was delivered to a medical facility. The Operations phase is followed by the Mission Conclusion phase in which SAR forces are returned and SAR case documentation completed.

Returning SAR forces entails releasing volunteered and commandeered units, such as *Discoverer*, from further Mayday responsibility and returning the dedicated SAR units, such as CG-1414, to their normal base of operations. SAR units are then normally debriefed, refueled, replenished, re-manned, and readied for other missions.

Entering the (successful) Completion Phase of the rescue effort meant that there was no further urgency in issuing case reports, so the messages transmitted over the next couple of days were of lower priority. They constitute a brief synopsis of the rescue although I did not read them until long after my return to land.

---

[132](...continued)

My best estimate is that the rafts floated into the Phoenix Island group, arriving there about the end of May or the first part of June. I hope that anyone who hears of a beautiful calico cat floating on to the shore of some tropical island on a big orange raft will let me know that she arrived safely.

The following pages summarize the successful search and rescue mission for *Haleakala*. They provide a brief examination of the SAR record. The reader who wants to get on with the story can skip to page 241.

Although these records are included to be helpful in passing on information to those who may become involved in a SAR mission, many other readers have found this picture of officialdom in a life-and-death situation both enlightening and entertaining. If you, the reader, would enjoy this counterpoint background, please continue.

The Mission Conclusion documentation in *Haleakala*'s case consisted mainly of the telexes starting with a report from *Discoverer*[133] sent just after she departed the disaster area.

By announcing to the Sar Mission Control Center that the (only) survivor had been recovered, *Discoverer* assumed responsibility for the care of the survivor and for his save delivery ashore. Rescue mission complete, *Discoverer* removed herself from further participation in the SAR mission.[134]

---

[133]Note that the report includes the fact that a radar reflector was placed on board the wreckage. Although the radar reflector seemed to me to be well placed on the rudder by the rescue party, subsequent tests of its effectiveness failed. It was unable to be detected by the ship's radar.

[134]*Discoverer* had now satisfied the SOLAS 1960 treaty obligations (see Footnote 50, 50 on page 80). The master of a vessel, be she in distress or not,

(continued...)

Document 22.
23 APR 1005Z (2305W) 11:05 p.m. Telex.

```
FROM NOAAS DISCOVERER
TO JRCC HONOLULU HI
SUBJECT: SAILING VESSEL HALEAKALA

1.  AT 23 APR 0922Z WE RECOVERED MR. CHARLES
    COLEMAN FROM THE OVERTURNED CATAMARAN
    HALEAKALA AT 00-21.3N 165-06.3W.

2.  UNABLE TO RECOVER CATAMARAN.  PLACED RADAR
    REFLECTOR ON BOARD AND LEFT STROBE LIGHTS ON
    BOARD.

3.  DEPARTED AREA ON COURSE 245 SEARCHING FOR
    TWO LIFE RAFTS ALONG WAY.  ONE LIFE RAFT
    CONTAINS MR. COLEMAN'S PET CAT.

4.  MR. COLEMAN APPEARS IN GOOD HEALTH.  WE HAVE
    PHYSICIAN ON BOARD AND WILL GIVE HIM PHYSICAL.

5.  PRESENTLY PLAN TO PUT MR. COLEMAN ASHORE IN
    HONOLULU.

7.  COAST GUARD FURNISHED EPIRB WAS REMOVED
    FROM VESSEL.  MR. COLEMAN'S EPIRB WAS INSIDE
    OVERTURNED HULL AND APPARENTLY STILL WORKING
    WHEN WE DEPARTED.

8.  ITS BEEN A PLEASURE TO JOIN YOU IN THIS OPERATION.
```

---

[134](...continued)
is the persona of the vessel and is frequently referred to by the name of the vessel. Therefore as the master and only survivor of *Haleakala*, by seeking refuge aboard *Discoverer*, I did, in fact, officially release her from further obligation to render assistance and continue aid to *Haleakala*, the vessel in distress.

Four hours after *Discoverer* had telexed the details of the successful rescue effort, and with no further on-site coordination needed, the JRCC designated themselves as continuing SAR Mission Coordinator for the Mission Conclusion Phase. In effect this action also canceling the on scene authority previously assigned to CG-1414 by point 4.B in the telex on page 111.

Document 23.
23 APR 1417Z (0417W) 4:17 a.m. Telex.

FROM JRCC
TO <SAR Forces>

SUBJECT: DISTRESS, SAILING VESSEL HALEAKALA
     SINKING

1. APR 0922Z NOAAS DISCOVERER ARRIVED ON STATION
   AND RECOVERED MR.CHARLES COLEMAN FROM
   SUBJECT VESSEL.

2. CASE CLOSED

3. JRCC DESIGNATED SAR MISSION COORDINATOR.

4. MULTI-UNIT CASE NUMBER ASSIGNED

The telex that officially closed the case was followed a longer report addressed to the 21 Air Force locations which had potential SAR assets for the mission.

Document 24.

23 APR 1835Z (0835W)   8:35 a.m. Telex (1 of 3).

FROM JRCC HONOLULU HI
TO <21 Air Force Locations>

SUBJECT: REPORT TO AIR FORCE RESOURCES

1. RESCUE CLOSING REPORT: CLOSED AT 23 APR 1442Z

2. MISSION NUMBER: PAC-014A-12 APR.

3. SITUATION: ASSISTING COAST GUARD DISTRICT-14 TO
   SEARCH FOR SAILING VESSEL HALEAKALA TAKING ON
   WATER ON TRIP FROM AMERICAN SAMOA TO
   HONOLULU HI.
   A.   PERSONNEL INFORMATION:
    1 INVOLVED, 1 LOCATED, 1 RECOVERED, 1 SAVED.
   B.   IDENTIFY LOCATING AGENCY:
    AIR FORCE C-141 (63 MAW) CG C-130 (CG 14 DIST).
   C.   IDENTIFY RECOVERY AGENCY & METHOD USED:
    NOAAS DISCOVERER, METHOD USED UNKNOWN.
   D.   DISPOSITION OF SAR OBJECTIVE:
    ON BOARD NOAAS DISCOVERER BOUND FOR
    HONOLULU HI.
    ESTIMATED TIME OF ARRIVAL OF DISCOVERER IS 1
    MAY.

4. FLYING ACTIVITY:
UNIT	SORTIES	HOURS
63 MAW C-141	1	11.1
CG DIST 14 C-130	2	9.3 TO DATE

NOTE USCG C-130 AT CHRISTMAS ISLAND. ESTIMATED
TIME OF ARRIVAL IN HONOLULU IS 23 APR.

5. SAVES DATA: 1 SAVE THIS MISSION.

Document 25.

23 APR 1835Z (0835W)   8:35 a.m. Telex (page 2 of 3).

---

6. FUTURE PLANS: MISSION CLOSED

7. SUMMARY OF SAR ACTIONS:

   A.   NARRATIVE DESCRIPTION OF SAR EFFORTS:

   SUBJECT VESSEL WAS RELOCATED BY CG-1414 AT
       POSITION 00-25N 164-59W AT 23 APR 0240Z.
   SURVIVOR ON BOARD IN GOOD CONDITION WITH
       MINOR CUTS AND BRUISES.
   BOAT IS TOTALLY INVERTED AND SEEMS TO BE
       RIDING WELL IN WATER.
   CG-1414 DROPPED RADIO CAN CONTAINING
       PORTABLE RADIO, 14 PEN GUN FLARES, 2
       DAY/NIGHT FLARES, FOOD, WATER, SPACE
       BLANKET AND JELLY BEANS WHICH WERE
       RECOVERED BY VICTIM.
   COMMUNICATIONS WERE ESTABLISHED WITH VICTIM
       AND DATUM MARKER BUOY DROPPED.
   COORDINATES WERE RELAYED TO NOAAS
       DISCOVERER, WHO PROCEEDED IN ROUTE TO
       RECOVER SUBJECT FROM VESSEL.
   QUELL 01, C-130 FROM 6594TH TEST GROUP FLEW
       TO AREA TO ESTABLISH COMMUNICATIONS
       WITH VICTIM UNTIL THE NOAAS DISCOVERER
       ARRIVED ON SCENE.
   23 APR 0922Z THE NOAAS DISCOVERER
       RECOVERED VICTIM.
   SHIP PHYSICIAN ON BOARD WILL GIVE VICTIM
       PHYSICAL.

Of particular interest from studying the details of this

Document 26.
23 APR 1835Z (0835W)   8:35 a.m. Telex (page 3 of 3).

```
┌────────────────────────────────────────────────────────┐
│                                                        │
│   B.  TOTAL FLYING ACTIVITY:                           │
│                                                        │
│          UNIT                SORTIES HOURS             │
│          63 MAW C-141              1      11.1         │
│          CG DIST 14 C-130          2       9.3         │
│          USAF 6594 TEST G C-130    1      11.1         │
│                                                        │
│   C.  AREA SEARCHED IN SQUARE MILES:                   │
│                                                        │
│          RELOCATION BY EPIRB                           │
│                                                        │
└────────────────────────────────────────────────────────┘
```

three page telex was the fact that a Datum Marker Buoy[135] was dropped during one of the passes while I was in contact with the Coast Guard C-130. (See the item under part 7 of page 2 of the telex.) The buoy is designed to be easily relocated anytime until the batteries eventually wear out. This time they either failed to provide the homing signal, or the rafts, and buoy, must have quickly separated from the derelict ship. Neither the rafts nor the buoy was ever located again.

By noon in Honolulu, the second and final Distress Situation Report Referring to the SAR case had been prepared and is reproduced as Document 27. Referring to that telex, the

---

[135]The Datum Marker Buoy device is a position indication radio buoy much like an EPIRB which is designed to maintain its relative position on the surface of the ocean to mark a site to track the motion of and/or to return to. The basic assumption for which it was used, is that the life rafts and wreckage would remain together in the same general vicinity and that the datum buoy would mark their collective position.

telex on page 187, and footnote 120 on page 184, the following actions probably took place:

Probable Chain of Events

22 APR 0145Z (1445X) 2:45 p.m. at the search area.[136]

CG-1414 arrived in the search area.

22 APR 0155Z (1455X) 2:55 p.m.

CG-1414 commenced an expanding square search pattern after having proceeded down the vessel dead reckoning drift for 25 miles at 150 knots.

22 APR 0230Z (1530X) 3:30 p.m.

CG-1414 abandoned the search less than an hour later and proceeded toward wreckage—because the EPIRB position could now be determined by the change in signal strength being measured during the expanded square search pattern execution.

22 APR 0245Z (1545X) 3:45 p.m.

Located wreckage and survivor.

---

[136]This is 3:45 p.m. in Honolulu. Note that the various time zones may add confusion to the time table which itself does not exactly match the referenced documents.

22 APR 0305Z (1605X) 4:05 p.m.

The plane departed at the very last minute for a pre-sunset landing at Christmas Island.

22 APR 0557Z (1757X) 5:57 p.m.

Coast Guard SAR Flight CG-1414 lands at Christmas Island three minutes before the nominal time for the sun to set!

End of Probable Chain of Events

The sharp eyed reader may notice subtle variations in different reported positions of the wreckage and survivor, in addition to the details of the various time tables on which the above scenario is reconstructed. The surface of the ocean is in constant motion and currents carry wreckage along with them. Nevertheless, some of the discrepancies are larger than would be that easily explained. These inaccuracies may give the reader a better appreciation of the difficulty of locating survivors.

Part of the Case closure includes a notification to mariners of the potential hazard of drifting wreckage even though the chance of hitting such wreckage is slim; note that *Haleakala*, herself, had indeed struck some form of flotsam.

Document 27.

23 APR 2216Z (1216W) 12:16 p.m. Telex.

FROM: JRCC HONOLULU HI
TO: <Coast Guard and recovery resources>

SUBJECT: DISTRESS SITUATION REPORT TWO AND FINAL
SAILING VESSEL HALEAKALA T.O.W.

1. SITUATION: AS BEFORE.

2. ACTION TAKEN:

A. 22 APR 2036Z CG-1414 DEPARTS COAST GUARD
AIR STATION BARBERS POINT IN ROUTE LAST REPORTED
POSITION OF SUBJECT VESSEL.

B. 23 APR 0145Z CG-1414 ON STATION, COMMENCED
EXPANDING SQUARE SEARCH AROUND LAST KNOWN
POSITION.

C. 23 APR 0240Z SUBJECT LOCATED PARTIALLY
SUBMERGED AND INVERTED. OWNER/OPERATOR IN GOOD
SHAPE, ABOARD.

D. 23 APR 0922Z NOAAS DISCOVERER ARRIVED ON
STATION, LOCATED VESSEL AND REMOVED
OWNER/OPERATOR. SUBJECT VESSEL REMAINS ADRIFT.

3. FUTURE PLANS:

A. ISSUE HYDROPAC REQUEST ON PARTIALLY
SUBMERGED DERELICT.

B. NOAAS DISCOVERER ESTIMATED TIME OF
ARRIVAL IN HONOLULU 1 MAY.

C. CASE CLOSED.

Discoverer would have been fully justified[137] in destroying the wreckage but the crew and I were grateful that she was spared. The disposition of the wreckage and the fate of the rafts both were potential topics to be addressed in a notice to mariners. Consequently, the JRCC requested the details for immediate publication.

By half past eight the next morning, Coast Guard plane, CG-1414, that had been forced to land before dark,[138] was again airborne on the way back to Hawaii. Even this brief stay in a foreign country required that they clear U.S. Customs when they returned.

The recovery vessel *Discoverer* had apparently responded to the midnight request for information for a notice to mariners because the text of the proposed notice was ready for transmission to the issuing agency (DMAHTC) the next morning.

A few minutes after CG-1414 had notified the JRCC that they were airborne from Christmas Island, thousands of miles away the notice to mariners was broadcast from Washington, DC. This notice was a significantly abbreviated form of the text

---

[137]Even *Discoverer* had a similar incident [hitting flotsam?] while they were in the deep South Pacific, a week or two before. One night the off-watch crew were shaken from their sleep by a loud bang which was accompanied by a sudden drop in the propeller shaft RPM's. Immediate investigation revealed no damage and no cause. At the next port of call, American Samoa, a detailed underwater survey for damage was undertaken but also revealed no damage and no explanation for the sound and sudden change in propeller shaft speed.

[138]Sunset always occurs very close to 6 p.m. (apparent local time) so close to the Equator and sunrise also occurs at 6 a.m. resulting in a twelve hour day and a twelve hour night.

Document 28.
23 APR 2251Z (1251W) 12:51 p.m. Telex.

```
FROM JRCC HONOLULU HI
TO NOAAS DISCOVERER

SUBJECT: DISTRESS S/V HALEAKALA SINKING

  1.  REQUEST FINAL DISPOSITION OF S/V HALEAKALA.

  2.  REQUEST STATUS OF LIFE RAFTS.

  3.  THIS INFO REQUESTED FOR NOTICE TO MARINERS OF
NAVIGATION HAZARD.
```

Document 29.
24 APR 1825Z (0825W) 8:25 a.m. Telex.

```
FROM CG-1414 CHRISTMAS ISLAND (VIA BARBERS POINT)
TO JRCC HONOLULU HI

SUBJECT: S/V HALEAKALA SINKING SAR CASE

  1.  24 APR 1902Z HC-130 CG-1414 LT J G FARROW
DEPARTS CHRISTMAS ISLAND IN ROUTE BARBERS POINT.
ESTIMATED TIME OF ARRIVAL IS 24 APR 2245Z.

  2.  REQUEST CUSTOMS AND AGRICULTURE INSPECTION
UPON ARRIVAL BARBERS PT.
```

suggested by the JRCC eight hours before.[139]

---

[139]The reader is invited to compare the suggested wording with the final text in Document 31. Noting that the final text is only half as long as that proposed by the Coast Guard Center in Honolulu.

Document 30.
24 APR 0508Z (1908W) 7:08 p.m. Telex.

FROM COAST GUARD 14TH DISTRICT HONOLULU HI
TO DMAHTC WASHINGTON DC

SUBJECT: HYDROPAC REQUEST NUMBER 021

1. REQUEST ISSUE HYDROPAC CENTRAL PACIFIC.

QUOTE.

THE S/V HALEAKALA A 56FT CATAMARAN WITH RED HULLS
AND A RADAR REFLECTOR WAS CAPSIZED AND
ABANDONED ADRIFT IN POSITION 00-20.7N 165-06.9W AT 23
APR 0900Z. THE VESSEL HAS AN EPIRB INSIDE HULL THAT
MAY BE TRANSMITTING ON 121.5 MHZ OR 243.0 MHZ. TWO
20 MAN ORANGE LIFE RAFTS WERE DEPLOYED IN THE
SAME POSITION AND HAVE NOT BEEN RECOVERED.

UNQUOTE.

2. CANCEL THIS HYDROPAC 26 APR 0430Z.

Document 31.
24 APR 1338Z (0838R) Washington, D.C., 8:38 a.m. Telex.

FROM DMAHTC WASHINGTON DC
TO AIG 4557

SUBJECT: HYDROPAC 540. CENTRAL PACIFIC

56 FOOT CATAMARAN HALEAKALA, EPIRB 121.5 MHZ OR
243.0 MHZ ON BOARD, ABANDONED AND CAPSIZED IN
00-20.7N 165-06.9W AT 23 APR 0900Z. REPORTS COAST
GUARD

Document 32.
24 APR 2050Z (1050W) 10:50 a.m. Telex.

FROM CENTRAL PACIFIC SAR COORDINATOR
TO NOAAS DISCOVERER

SUBJECT: S/V HALEAKALA SINKING

1. THE TIMELY ASSISTANCE PROVIDED BY YOU AND YOUR
CREW TO THE MASTER OF THE CATAMARAN HALEAKALA
IS NOTED WITH GREAT PLEASURE. WORKING SKILLFULLY
WITH RESCUE AIRCRAFT, YOU RECOVERED MR CHARLES
COLEMAN FROM HIS STRICKEN VESSEL ON THE NIGHT OF
22 APRIL, PROVIDED HIM WITH MEDICAL CARE, AND
COMPASSIONATELY ALLOWED HIM A PHONE PATCH WITH
HIS LOVED ONES

2. AS IS SO OFTEN THE CASE, A NOAA VESSEL HAS
WILLINGLY AND SELFLESSLY PROVIDED A HUMANITARIAN
SERVICE WHICH FOLLOWS THE HIGHEST TRADITIONS OF
MARINERS AT SEA

3. WELL DONE.

SIGNED CAPT A C TINGLEY, ACTING CENTRAL PACIFIC SAR
COORDINATOR

The message of commendation to *Discoverer* recognizes her service to maritime community and particularly to one man in maximum peril in the sea.

Early that afternoon, the Coast Guard at Barbers Point notified the JRCC that CG-1414 had landed. After flight CG-1414 had flown the five hours back to Oahu, all activated

SAR forces had been returned and all released from further participation in the mission.

Document 33.

25 APR 0001Z (1401W) 2:01 p.m. Telex.

FROM COAST GUARD BARBERS POINT
TO JRCC HONOLULU HI

SUBJECT: S/V HALEAKALA SINKING

1. 24 APR 2259Z HC-130 CG-1414 ARRIVED AT BARBERS POINT. MISSION COMPLETE.

2. SAR STATISTICS: 1 MISSION, 1 SORTIE, 5.0 HRS FLOWN.

The active SAR mission was now complete and only additional debriefing, documentation, and preparation for future missions remained. The concluding two documents that follow are the official special commendation to the rescue unit, the NOAA *Discoverer*, and a general commendation to all the participating forces.

The final telex to all SAR Forces was sent two days after the congratulatory telex to *Discoverer*. I had already been able to express my thanks to the "Disco Family," as they refer to themselves. I circulated a note of thanks and they returned a letter of welcome signed by all aboard.

Document 34.
26 APR 1646Z (0646W) 6:46 a.m. Telex.

FROM CENTRAL PACIFIC SAR COORDINATOR
TO <SAR Forces>

SUBJECT: DISTRESS S/V HALEAKALA TAKING ON WATER

1. THE RAPID RESPONSE AND PROFESSIONALISM
DISPLAYED BY ALL PARTICIPANTS IS NOTED WITH
PLEASURE. YOUR COMBINED EFFORT CONTRIBUTED
DIRECTLY TO THE SAVING OF A LIFE IMPERILED IN A
REMOTE PORTION OF THE PACIFIC. ESPECIALLY WORTHY
OF MENTION IS THE CREW OF MAC-38084, WHO ON
SHORT NOTICE AND OUTSIDE THE REALM OF EXPECTED
MISSION REQUIREMENTS FOR A C-141, DELIVERED THREE
INFLATABLE LIFE RAFTS TO THE STRICKEN VESSEL WITH
REMARKABLE ACCURACY. THE VESSEL'S MASTER WAS
TAKEN ABOARD THE NOAAS DISCOVERER ON THE NIGHT
OF 22 APRIL AND IS PRESENTLY IN ROUTE HONOLULU
HAVING SUFFERED NO APPARENT ILL EFFECTS FROM HIS
ORDEAL.

2. TAKE PRIDE IN YOUR HUMANITARIAN EFFORT. THANK
YOU FOR A JOB WELL DONE.

CAPT. A. C. TINGLEY, ACTING CENTRAL PACIFIC SAR
COORDINATOR, SENDS

Honolulu Aloha

The excitement grew throughout the crew as we approached Honolulu. Many of those aboard, including myself, would leave the ship in Honolulu. Leaving port to set sail is always exciting but arrival even more so. As the miles to shore begin to shrink, small boat sailors start dreaming of whatever they miss most while at sea: maybe an ice cold beer, maybe a steak, maybe ice cream. I found most often my craving while nearing port, was for the fresh fruit and vegetables which are lacking on small boats at sea.

On the last day, well before dawn, I was on the bridge of *Discoverer* looking at the charts and instruments and projecting our time of arrival. Now rather than fresh fruit and vegetables, I was desperately craving a Honolulu aloha from Elli. I also was thinking how nearly I had widowed her. I was to find out later how I nearly lost her just before our arrival.

Elli knew we were to arrive at Aloha Tower and the expected time of our arrival. For a large ship the expected time is usually very close to the actual time. Nevertheless, anxious and restless with anticipation, she was up very early and started for Aloha Tower well before we were due to enter the harbor. Aloha Tower, a waterfront landmark, was "the" place to arrive in the days of exclusive ocean travel to Hawaii, and it is still used by cruise ships calling at Honolulu.

Making her way to the Tower while the streets were still relatively quiet, she stood waiting for the green light as she considered the best vantage point to watch the ship enter the harbor. When she got the "WALK" sign and started across, a car waiting to make a right turn, the driver watching intently for traffic from the left, also started moving just as she left the curb. He saw her at the last moment and stopped, in time while giving them both a bad scare.[140]

We were still out of sight of Aloha Tower at the time of Elli's near accident. A small craft advisory had been in effect for several days as we approached Honolulu. Now the weather had calmed with the typical scattered tropical squalls and no major stormy areas. While for many days we had been alone in the sea, now the ocean traffic increased noticeably. Several fishing boats were heading out to deeper water. An ocean tug was towing an unusual looking barge out to sea. Clouds hung on the mountains in the dim light of approaching dawn. The clouds changed to morning high-mountain mist in the background as La, the sun god, rose from the sea. The large buildings of downtown Honolulu took shape, and the familiar skyline of Waikiki cleared from the mist.

As we got ever closer, more and more familiar sights appeared. We were close enough to identify the individual buildings in downtown Honolulu as they grew in size. Finally we entered the harbor clearly marked by Aloha Tower.

---

[140]It is certainly true that at times the danger of crossing the street can be equal to the danger of single-handing across a vast ocean. Elli and I have mused how impossibly tragic it would have been had I lost HER to a common traffic accident after finally having myself been rescued in spite of the tremendous odds against any such rescue at sea!

I looked all over the water front below the Tower searching for Elli but could not see her in the distance. Going out on the upper deck to see better as well as to be seen better, I heard her calling. She was high up in the Tower near the big clock waving frantically, and I waved and shouted back as *Discoverer* came alongside the dock and mooring lines were made fast.

How long ago it seemed that I had left Pago Pago on *Haleakala*. Now she had foundered, and I was left with only my orange can and the generous gifts of clothes donated by the crew of *Discoverer*. But, most importantly, together Elli and I still had a future before us. In my happiness I never even considered for a moment the material loss we had suffered. After all, my single most important possession, my life, had been saved!

I had no idea of the amount of red tape that was descending upon me. The very first problem was getting off of the ship! I had the feeling of a man without a country, and all I was trying do was see my wife.

U.S. Immigration Service regulations quarantine a ship, detaining <u>all</u> passengers, until <u>every</u> passenger and crew has been cleared into the country. All passengers and crew must wait aboard and all friends and relatives ashore until the paperwork is completed.[141]

---

[141]This procedure seems reasonable at face value. However, this governmental power to make border crossing difficult has reached quite unbelievable extremes in the actions of some petty minded official representatives. Waiting for many hours in line to pass through customs gates

(continued...)

This absolute quarantine meant no one was to be allowed to enter or leave the ship until I, the very last person to be examined,[142] was cleared. But in order for me to enter the country, they insisted I had to either produce my passport or "other acceptable proof of citizenship." I had not thought to take my passport and wallet as essential "survival" gear in the last few moments before I very nearly lost my life. The captain's certification that I had been plucked from a foundered U.S. documented vessel in mid ocean en route from an American port did not seem to carry much weight with the inspecting agents.

The ship and personnel were finally allowed reunion with their waiting family and friends when I was "allowed" a Conditional Entry Permit with the requirement that I present proof of citizenship at the Honolulu immigration office within a few days. It was futile pointing out that my lost passport was issued by the Honolulu office of the State Department and my passport picture should be on file there, and that I was in the Hawaiian Department of Motor Vehicle files having held a Hawaii drivers license.

Getting new identification is a "Catch 22" situation. You have to have identification in order to get identification! Obviously I was able to reestablish my identity, but it was a long

---

[141](...continued)

into the United States is well documented by irate foreign national tourists. The lack of effectiveness of these extremely annoying procedures in achieving their objective, to stem the flow of illegal drugs into the country, is equally well documented.

[142]Even the order in which the passengers, officers, crew, and survivor were examined was probably the least efficient order possible.

244

and arduous undertaking as the wheels of bureaucracy grind slowly and in mysterious ways. One passport office employee expressed surprise that I had not been fined for "entering the country without a passport." I'm glad that they didn't mention this at the time I arrived. I also hadn't taken money with me as additional "survival gear" in order to pay the fine.

Survivor Debriefing

Safely ashore in Honolulu (at last), I called the Coast Guard to thank them and to offer a survivor debriefing. I also asked for a copy of my SAR case file to satisfy my curiosity as to what had happened behind the scenes to affect my rescue. In response, I was invited to the center to relate my experiences. Elli and I were welcomed by Captain Lucas, Commanding Officer of the JRCC, who gave us a copy of the SAR file.

Several aboard *Discoverer* had encouraged me to document my survival. Realizing that documentation takes a considerable amount of time, I did not want to delay. The offer for immediate debriefing was made in hopes that others could profit from my mistakes and any insights I might have about the rescue effort. Many of the aspects of the rescue discussed in these pages became apparent only much later, after I had the opportunity to carefully read the SAR case file. My comments at the debriefing mainly concerned my errors, the survival materials, and the treatment of a capsized multi-hull.

First, even before starting repairs, once I knew *Haleakala* was seriously damaged, I should have taken the time to launch the dinghy and put survival supplies aboard. The time it would have taken would not have kept me from repairing the hole, and I could easily have brought it back aboard later if the repairs were successful. As it was, I lost access to the dinghy and supplies when the vessel capsized.

Second, trying to prevent capsize should have been my major concern since I did not need to fear sinking. Unfortunately, I did not think of what I should have done to prevent it until immediately after the capsize. When I found the port amidship flooding to be more extensive than I had realized, I should have INCREASED the damage! If I had made a second, larger hole in the opposite, undamaged hull, I would have been able to maintain trim. It would have meant sinking down to the wing bottom twice as fast with double the damage to repair, but *Haleakala* would have remained *upright*, and I would have had all the time I needed to affect repairs with all the repair materials and survival supplies readily available. Incidentally, no yachtsman I have told my story to since has offered this advice although Navy officers, trained in maintaining ship stability, have seen this alternative immediately.

And, finally, *under no circumstances* should I have abandoned the boat for the raft. The lure of the life raft was nearly fatal, and swimming for it I consider my major error. I had violated my own rule to "always stay with the boat." The unsinkable multi-hull is its own survival platform, and ordinary life rafts *without supplies* are of no great value to survivors on an overturned multi-hull. Survivors on catamarans and trimarans

246

may be in desperate need of *communication and supplies*, and these, not rafts, *should be the priority* for air drops to multihulls.

I consider my ham radio, SATNAV, and EPIRB the electronic instruments most crucial to my rescue. The ham radio let me communicate my disaster situation; the SATNAV instantaneously gave me an accurate position to report; and the EPIRB was used to locate me, although only with marginal success after the search was underway. The intended use of an EPIRB to alert passing aircraft and then SAR forces, failed in my case.

I was quite surprised to learn that the EPIRB left aboard *Haleakala* was eventually heard by a passing commercial airliner in route to Australia.

I was more angry than surprised to learn that the pilot did not report reception of the EPIRB signal for an additional *week* after it was heard!

I would hope for all survivors that EPIRB receptions would be reported in minutes not days.

Of the survival equipment that was dropped to me, I was most grateful for the EPIRB *with two-way communication* capability. The inability to communicate had been a major problem. Water and food were the next most valuable items for survival although I could have survived for several days more without them. Opening them would have been a problem without my knife, in the absence of a can opener, but I'm sure I would have found a way. I suggested pop-top cans be considered for water and food although there is a question about the long term stability of a pop-top. A survival knife might also be a valuable tool to be included in survival gear, particularly if pop-top cans cannot tolerate long storage times. The greatest disappointment was the survival blanket, and I returned a shredded piece to illustrate the point.

My last point about survival equipment concerned the use of an olive drab background behind the black lettering of instructions and labels. Such low contrast background makes the lettering illegible at night without some steady light source such as a flashlight. The included strobe light was too brief and blinding for use in reading the labels. While the inability to read the instructions after dark did not endanger me, I suggested the black lettering of all survival gear instructions and labeling be put on a day-glow orange background and/or a small flashlight included as part of survival supplies.

The only important operational suggestion I had to offer at the time I talked to Captain Lucas concerned the treatment of a capsized multi-hull. It is safe to assume all modern trimarans and catamarans cannot sink. While a mono-hull relies on ballast for stability, a multi-hull achieves stability from the multiple hulls. And because they are usually constructed of floating materials and/or with additional flotation installed, multihulls are intrinsically unsinkable; their primary safety factor.

The use of multiple hulls instead of ballast for stability also leads to a safety problem. A properly designed, ballasted monohull can right itself if knocked down or even turned completely over (a "three-sixty") providing it is not also flooded. However the multihull has a second stable position, upside down, which constitutes the major multihull safety problem.

248

Unfortunately, *Haleakala* assumed the second stable position. (Additional analysis of multihull stability is appropriate but beyond the scope of this book.)

I offered a possible different technique for dropping supplies to victims in the water, either adrift or in rafts; I suggested using two parachutes, one tied to each end of a long floating polypropylene line with the survival can fastened in the middle.

This suggestion was based on a safety technique I used for swimming parties at sea. Before anyone was permitted in the water, about 150 feet of half-inch polypropylene line was dropped over the side with the bitter-end belayed to a cleat. Even though hove-to, the boat would drift somewhat but the line would always be trailing back on the surface from whichever direction the boat had moved. A swimmer could catch the line and pull himself to safety if the boat started to drift too far away.

Lastly, I mentioned the "drifting" speed of *Haleakala*. I explained she was making headway up weather. Although no one challenged my contention, I don't think they supported the idea either. All of the drifting speed data that had been studied and graphed in the SAR Manual shows only an amount of leeway indicating the wind always carries things down-wind and at increasing speed as the wind speed increases. Perhaps if I had supported my observation with the "disappearing whale" analogy at the time, the observation might have been more believable.

We went over several more points which we discussed in reference to figures in the National Search and Rescue Manual. I remember discussing the SAR Regions and being told they knew of *no successful rescue further away from a SAR base*. The proof was apparent when a SAR operational limits map was brought out showing that the reported mayday of *Haleakala* was *on* the operational-limit line. If I had been over-the-line ... ?

I tried to personally thank as many of the SAR people as I could. Captain Lucas expressed his appreciation for my coming by and sharing my observations. Most survivors are probably so happy to be alive that they don't think of offering their experience to help others. He described my recovery as a "textbook case" of search and rescue. Although many SAR missions are launched, distressingly few are successful.

Captain Lucus told me: "I knew we were going to succeed when you fired the flare. *You* made your rescue possible."

Epilogue

A rather extensive analysis of the rescue effort was prepared for inclusion at the end of this book. Much additional data were amassed including physical facts and human insights, and even errors in judgement which occurred before as well as during the Search and Rescue Mission. I felt that sailors in general, and SAR forces in particular would be especially interested in greater detail. Sailors might gain knowledge and insights that would increase their chances of surviving a shipwreck while SAR forces might get a new perspective from a victim's point of view, for use on future missions.

Most of the material in these last sections was subsequently deleted as being of little interest to the majority of readers. Those who are particularity interested in pursuing more of this detail are invited to contact the author.

However, the material in two of these areas seems to be of sufficient interest and importance to be addressed here. The first area concerns electronic aids to search and rescue efforts and particularity the accuracy and reliability of the SATNAV and the trust it merits from blue water sailors. The second area, addressed in somewhat greater detail, concerns the psychological reactions that are common in a survival situation.

The SATNAV in Search and Rescue

The SATNAV can consistently determine a fix that is accurate to a fraction of a nautical mile whenever a navigation satellite passes overhead. Between fixes, the SATNAV maintains position by dead reckoning. Therefore, the accuracy of a SATNAV position can diminish as time goes by until another satellite passes overhead and a new fix is established. This dead reckoning by course and time is usually quite accurate, unless some major course change is made without updating the SATNAV. My heaving-to in order to assess and repair damage was just such a major course change, and without an electronic interface between the SATNAV and the ship's compass and log (to measure direction and speed), the SATNAV needed manual intervention.

I now conclude that the SATNAV continued to dead reckon the position by course and time and predicted a position further along the line from Pago Pago to Honolulu than we had actually sailed at the time I read the figures. What I should have done when COMMSTA asked for my position, was to include the indicated course, speed, and time of last fix from the SATNAV.[143]

---

[143] My expected position was some five miles east southeast of my reported position as plotted. But by the instrumentation aboard the plane, I had drifted 18 nautical miles south southwest. This calculates to a two and a quarter knot drift, an unusually large number. But even more unusual was the direction. My reported weather observation, including wind direction and speed, combined with the average ocean current, predict a position 15 miles north of that shown by the instruments aboard MAC-38084. Since neither the wind nor current were going south, the discrepancy had to be somewhere else.

(continued...)

Will-to-die versus Will-to-survive

The first hand experience in facing imminent death has brought me to an appreciation of appropriate survival reactions. What has been quite surprising to me is the preponderance of inappropriate survival reactions that are cited in the literature.[144]

Given the will to die, people generally have the inherent ability to commit suicide. But, why do people take this final alternative when rescue is possible, or later when rescue is at hand, and most amazingly, sometimes even after rescue has been *successful!*? Shipwreck victims have avoided potential rescuers rather than signalling them. Survivors have committed suicide

---

[143](...continued)

In addition to the ever present possibility of human error and the lesser probability of instrumentation error, a proper explanation of this discrepancy might make it easier to locate others adrift in the sea. I now attribute the error to the position I reported from my SATNAV. However, it should also have been possible for someone else to predict this error in order to establish a SAR search pattern with a higher probability of success than that which was initially established.

A SATNAV system is a wonderful piece of machinery but like all instruments, it has its own limitations. Prudent navigators do not rely on any one single navigation instrument. However, when an instrument proves to be extremely accurate and reliable, it is easy to forget those limitations and to put unwarranted trust in a "friend."

[144]A detailed review of the literature is beyond the scope of this book but the reader who wants to further understand survivor psychology is referred to "The Mental Factor" by John W. P. Leach, appearing in the Ocean Navigator (No. 47, page 79-87) and from which data were extracted for this epilogue.

while rescues are in process. In fact, after being rescued, victims have asked their attending physicians and nurses to help them commit suicide! To me, this is astonishing.

Most of my earlier information about survival psychology was based on anecdotes and passed by word of mouth among sailors. A yachtsman said goodbye and slipped over the side of the life raft to "swim away." Potential survivors "hid" on the floor of their life raft so that they wouldn't be seen from the passing ship. Such stories are passed on by those who supposedly witnessed the irrational behavior, but did not join in and therefore survived. But, indeed, there is more concrete evidence that these anecdotes suggest.

Although survival while emersed in cold water may be limited to few hours by hypothermia (as discussed briefly before), there is no particular danger of hypothermia in the shelter of a life raft. Nevertheless, a number of the passengers of the *Titanic*, picked up out of lifeboats within three hours of her sinking, and without apparent bodily harm, were already dead. Others who were in the same lifeboats were insane.

SAR data shows that a stationary (resting, not walking) person can survive seven days without water in the desert in temperatures reaching 90°F in the shade. Contrast this fact with a 1953 study that showed that 90% of shipwreck survivors die within three days, less than half the time expected under the more severe desert conditions. The inescapable conclusion is that these people exercised their will-to-die.

In stark contrast to the 90% dead in three days, we have the story *Adrift: Seventy-six days lost at sea* by Steve Callahan in which he tells how he survives, starting with only three pounds of food and eight pints of water. Steve proved that he could conquer, as he said, "The Witch and Her Curse: Hunger and Thirst." This he did with courage and determination, summed up as the will-to-live even while facing almost insurmountable hardships. Steve kept going, never stopping, even continuing to push himself as his physical condition deteriorated until he weighed about half his normal weight. Why was Steve different from those that succumb? His sailing and navigating skills were no different than could be expected of any sailor accustomed to solo ocean crossings. What makes his feat stand out is his great psychological strength.

Psychologists now tell us that there is a normal pattern of reaction to a disaster: shock and trauma of the event (from impact until aboard a life raft), recoil and analysis or denial (safe in the life raft but need to be rescued), and post-trauma anxiety and guilt (after the rescue when the total impact of the disaster hits home). Although this is a general pattern of reaction, there are both normal and abnormal (common and uncommon) actions and reactions in each of the three stages. I, too, went through these stages and my actions and reactions make more sense now in the context of the expected pattern.

The most common (75%) reaction to the trauma is a stunned bewilderment in which reasoning is greatly impaired. People operate in an automatic way, if at all, and disbelief and denial are common. A small number (12%) remain active but with inappropriate or irrational behavior, typically raging or weeping. A few (13%) remain calm (some remarkably so) and are able to assess the situation and plan for survival. My actions to the trauma have already been addressed in detail. I made a major mistake in judgement at this time (responding to the lure of the rafts) but I was also able to make plans (for getting back

255

to the wreckage) during this same trauma phase. If I had been more aware of the particular danger of faulty judgement in this phase, I might have been able to avoid my major mistake.

The recoil and analysis phase is one in which survivors, even those that were previously incapacitated by the trauma, separate out from the non-survivor class. Survivors return to or continue an awareness and use their reasoning ability to plan for survival. That was my reaction. Non-survivors show denial and apathy and spend time on irrelevant or counter-productive tasks.

The post-trauma period is one in which people often show signs and symptoms of psychiatric illness. The full impact of the disaster falls on the person and bereavement, depression, and guilt are common. Studies have shown that the great majority (one study showing over 95%) of survivors are in need of professional psychiatric help after rescue. While I was again in the minority, in not needing counseling, the writing of this book has been of similar value to me. I hope the reading of this book will be of equal value to you.

Would a friend enjoy reading this book?
Cut out this page to send them an announcement,
or surprise them with a copy - call (800) 247-6553.

Word Professionals Publishing
Honolulu, Hawaii

Announces

MAYDAY!
MAYDAY!   *TO:*
MAYDAY!
This is the *Haleakala*

by Charles Coleman

Adventure Autobiography Sailing Survival

In one of the most remote parts of the Pacific Ocean a small dot floated nearly invisible in the moonless black night. As dawn approached, tropical squalls further obscured this dot, now barely visible even a few feet away. No one was there to see that this dot was a man's head bobbing just above the surface of the inky black water of the desolate Central Pacific.

Adrift for hours, he had been working on the problem of how to survive. No life raft, no water, no food, no supplies, in fact, not even the wreckage of the *Haleakala* remained in the empty sea around him. Any hope of rescue depended on his experience, intelligence, and most importantly, his innate spirit.

Totally alone, as few people have been alone; stranded in the middle of the ocean hundreds of miles from islands and people; well over one thousand miles from the nearest rescue center; he floated, awaiting sunrise, knowing this was most likely his last dawn.

Charley never recognized the word *"impossible."* Although shipwrecked and adrift, he accepted the challenge to survive as the greatest and most crucial test of his life.

What he did and what others did to make ultimate rescue possible against all odds is this enthralling story of survival.

Orders: (800) 247-6553
FAX: (419) 281-6883

ISBN 0-9634022-1-8